PLAYS BY ALLAN HAVIS

BROADWAY PLAY PUBLISHING INC.

357 W 20th St., NY NY 10011
212 627-1055

First printing: July 1989
ISBN: 0-88145-071-5

Design by Marie Donovan
Word processing done in WordMarc Composer Plus. Set in Palatino using Xerox Ventura Publisher.
Printed on acid-free paper and bound in the United States of America.

CONTENTS

ABOUT THE AUTHOR

Allan Havis, whose works include HAUT GOÛT, THE LADIES OF FISHER COVE, LILITH, THE ROAD FROM JERUSALEM, and A SPECIAL AGENT, has seen his plays produced at South Coast Repertory, Hartford Stage, Virginia Stage, American Repertory Theatre, Ensemble Studio Theatre, The Philadelphia Theater Company, and in London. In New York, he has directed his plays off-Broadway at WPA, West Bank Cafe, and BACA.

MOROCCO received the 1985 FDG/CBS Award, the 1986 Playwrights USA Award from HBO, a 1987 Kennedy Center/American Express Grant, and was previously published in TCG's Anthology *New Plays USA 3*. HAUT GOÛT was seen last year at South Coast Repertory and subsequently published by TCG.

Mr. Havis is also the author of *ALBERT THE ASTRONOMER*, a children's novel published by Harper & Row. In the last three years he has been assisted by major grants, including a New York State Foundation for the Arts Fellowship and fellowships from the National Endowment for the Arts, and the Rockefeller, McKnight, and Guggenheim Foundations. His residencies include Robert Redford's Sundance Institute, the Edward Albee Foundation, the MacDowell Colony, New York's Public Theatre, and a 1988 Hawthornden Fellowship in Scotland. At present he is working on two commissions, from South Coast Repertory and New York's CSC Rep. Mr. Havis serves on the Graduate Theater Faculty at the University of California, San Diego and holds an MFA from the Yale School of Drama.

PRODUCTION NOTES

A common thread linking MOROCCO, MINK SONATA, and HOSPITALITY is the move away from naturalistic theater and American realism. These plays don't require a decorative approach with encroaching set design and ambient activities. I wrote these works from a distilled, elliptical perspective, and I would hope they would be interpreted accordingly.

The director who wishes to help the audience "enter" these plays ought to resist the common practice of literalisms and unnecessary pedantic logic. I believe each of these plays functions like half-real dreams, asking strictly for an inner logic. Leaps in action and narrative advance inner logic. Things need to be intuited before reasoned. When confronted with a choice between more clutter or less, it is best to clear the stage entirely. The language of these plays calls for strong rhythmic responses, hinting at deeply felt inner tensions and the obligatory mysterious subtext. The subtexts may vary, as they tend to do from production to production, but the tensions of deception remain the same. These plays involve the illusory aberration of truth and keen psychological gamesmanship. Devaluing any play's mystery to flat realism would be a great loss to the work. I cannot stress this enough.

A note about passion: These plays must convey intelligent, obsessive emotions. Be it Kempler's compulsive struggles with the Colonel and with his wife in MOROCCO, Roberta's dark inner battle with her alter-ego in MINK SONATA, or Happy's perverse interrogation techniques covered by mock insouciance in HOSPITALITY, an edgy, desperate energy should be evident to each character and to the respective situation. Moreover, though each play is uniquely disturbing, an element of wit is essential, from both the director and the cast. Word and posture should be poised for repartee and the unexpected reversal. Let the perverse irony ring boldly.

And finally, a note for the reader: Imagine these plays performed with all the accuracy, lyricism, and brio of concert music.

I believe it was Strindberg who said our race created language to keep secrets.

MOROCCO

ORIGINAL PRODUCTIONS

One-act version, American Repertory Theater, Cambridge MA, April 1984:

KEMPLER . . . . Tony Shaloub
COLONEL . . . . Ben Halley Jr.

Director . . . . Gerald Chapman

World premiere full-length version, Virginia Stage Company, Norfolk VA, first performance 27 February 1985:

KEMPLER . . . . Larry Pine
COLONEL . . . . Ray Aranha
MRS. KEMPLER . . . . Gordana Rashovich
WAITER . . . . Edward Morgan

Director . . . . Chris Hanna

New York premiere, WPA Theater, first performance 28 June 1988:

KEMPLER . . . . Sam Freed
COLONEL . . . . George Guidall
MRS. KEMPLER . . . . Gordana Rashovich
WAITER . . . . Anthony Ruiz

Director . . . . Allan Havis

PLAYWRIGHT'S NOTE

As if in a dream, MOROCCO travels an irregular path between things of certainty and doubt. The traditional notion of plot, admittedly, has fallen by the wayside. Time may be truncated or stretched in a particular subjected manner. Logic bends to one's displeasure. During moments of anxiety, reality fools us. Something may seem unreal, or far worse—hyperbolic. To inhabit a Max Ernst canvas for a day, a week, a month, would be most frightening. And yet, there is a comic afterthought to this cold, clammy sweat.

An American discovers that he is in a foreign land, without clear purpose or credentials, and in growing conflict with his better instincts. He pretends that, perhaps, the next morning will be brighter. Naked, his speech is distilled and terse. He stands at a threshold.

CHARACTERS

MR.KEMPLER—*An architect in his late thirties, working for a New York firm with clandestine contracts overseas. He is punctual, fastidious, and somewhat arrogant. His anger is slow to surface, although he manages to go through the motions. He is affluent, with experience in business kickbacks. He has been married for ten years and travels with his wife.*

COLONEL—*A much older man of Arab nationality. He has never seen foreign duty. Overweight and a chain smoker, he gives the appearance of an anxious man about to retire. His position is senior officer at a Moroccan jail for women. His sense of irony is broad and he cannot stifle a bad joke. He thinks his life could improve with a little luck. He deals with whores, drug dealers, and thieves. He takes pride in his difficult exterior. He has yet to arrest an American in his city.*

MRS. KEMPLER—*An unusually alluring woman in her mid-thirties. She is part Latin, part Arabian. Educated in England, she has only a slight Mediterranean accent. She hides very little about herself, but answers all pointed questions as though she were a day-born child. The cleverness inside her is unassuming and soft, and emerges in casual tones.*

WAITER

TIME

The present year.

PLACE

ACT ONE: *Fez, Morocco*

ACT TWO: *Malaga, Spain*

ACT THREE: *Fez, Morocco*

ACT ONE

(Fez, Morocco. The COLONEL*'s office inside the jailhouse.)*

DAY ONE

COLONEL: Is this a picture of your wife?

KEMPLER: Yes, I believe so.

COLONEL: And her wardrobe?

KEMPLER: I don't recognize it.

COLONEL: And have you seen these? *(More photos)*

KEMPLER: I don't quite understand.

COLONEL: *(Pause)* Please, have a seat.

KEMPLER: Is she here?

COLONEL: Yes. *(Offering a cigarette)*

KEMPLER: No, thanks. I don't smoke.

COLONEL: I understand you are an architect.

KEMPLER: Yes.

COLONEL: That's quite impressive. Working very hard?

KEMPLER: Yes.

COLONEL: Work is wonderful for the spirit.

KEMPLER: I'm sure.

COLONEL: It says in my report that your wife is a banker.

KEMPLER: That is correct.

COLONEL: An executive?

KEMPLER: Yes.

COLONEL: We treat bankers very well.

KEMPLER: How kind of you.

COLONEL: Do I cause you great embarrassment, Mr. Kempler?

KEMPLER: Not at all.

COLONEL: Wives sometime misbehave.

KEMPLER: You must have confused her with someone else.

COLONEL: I don't believe so.

KEMPLER: Are you head of staff?

COLONEL: Colonel, yes.

KEMPLER: Perhaps you can tell me why she was apprehended.

COLONEL: Certainly. *(Pause)* Prostitution, disorderly conduct, drunkenness.

KEMPLER: That's absurd.

COLONEL: *(Amused)* Of course. *(Pause)* And you wish to post bail?

KEMPLER: Yes, naturally.

COLONEL: I think we can arrange something. *(Pause)* Your wife spent last night sleepless.

KEMPLER: Is she all right?

COLONEL: Reasonable well.

KEMPLER: When may I see her?

COLONEL: Shortly. She's now with our medics.

KEMPLER: She was kept in a cell last night?

COLONEL: Yes.

KEMPLER: Why wasn't I phoned earlier?

COLONEL: She was in no condition to be released. Our buildings are sanitary, Mr. Kempler.

KEMPLER: May I use your telephone?

COLONEL: I'd rather you didn't.

KEMPLER: Colonel, I find these charges incredible to believe.

COLONEL: Yes, I can sympathize.

KEMPLER: Abril doesn't drink.

COLONEL: Perhaps there is more about her.

KEMPLER: I think not.

COLONEL: May I ask you something, Mr. Kempler? *(Pause)* Why are you here?

KEMPLER: In Morocco?

COLONEL: Yes.

KEMPLER: Our jobs brought us here.

COLONEL: Please make it clear to me.

KEMPLER: You have our papers.

COLONEL: Is it that you like foreign food?

KEMPLER: Our work coincides often, and so we travel. My firm is building the industrial park outside your city.

COLONEL: Yes, I know that.

KEMPLER: Abril is with the Affiliate Bank.

COLONEL: Does she dress this way at the office?

KEMPLER: Obviously not.

COLONEL: Do they not pay her enough?

KEMPLER: Please don't sound ridiculous.

COLONEL: Do I?

KEMPLER: It is a gross distortion.

COLONEL: There is a serious epidemic in my country, and some precautions are needed.

KEMPLER: I can understand.

COLONEL: Not that we don't want foreign investors.

KEMPLER: Then why pick on my wife?

COLONEL: May I recite a parable? *(Phone rings; answering phone.)*
Na-on? (yes) *(Listening)* Sho-kun. (thank you) *(To* KEMPLER*)* Your
wife had been checked for a contagion. She will be detained.

KEMPLER: You must let me see her.

COLONEL: For now that must wait.

KEMPLER: I insist.

COLONEL: You should make a friend of me, Mr. Kempler. I am in a
position to help you.

KEMPLER: I'm listening.

COLONEL: First, have a cigarette. *(*KEMPLER *accepts one.)* You needn't
inhale to enjoy.

KEMPLER: What can I do for you?

COLONEL: *(Ignoring* KEMPLER*)* The tobacco is excellent. Almost sweet.

KEMPLER: Yes, very mild.

COLONEL: I keep them in a humidor.

KEMPLER: Very wise.

COLONEL: And yet my wife worries for me. Cancer scares.

KEMPLER: Can I write a check?

COLONEL: No, no, no. I wasn't looking for a gift, Mr. Kempler. First
of all, my commander would expect a percentage. Secondly, I would
feel compromised and obligated. You might send other things in the
mail. I could not in good conscience accept anything in this context.
No, no, keep your checks. You are in the company of an honest
officer.

KEMPLER: That is reassuring.

COLONEL: Furthermore, a bribe is a direct insult to Morocco.

KEMPLER: Colonel, I was not suggesting anything of the kind.

COLONEL: Bribes make soldiers complacent. Am I repeating myself?
(Pause) Please, put aside your checkbook. We will do this the proper
way.

KEMPLER: Fine.

COLONEL: Do you play chess?

KEMPLER: Why do you ask?

COLONEL: I am quite skillful at the game. And backgammon. Do you play backgammon, Mr. Kempler?

KEMPLER: No.

COLONEL: Four-handed bridge?

KEMPLER: No, Colonel.

COLONEL: Did you play with little buildings as a boy?

KEMPLER: Please, we're wasting time.

COLONEL: Yes, I am sorry. *(Pause)* How is it that you married a whore?

KEMPLER: I will call the U.S. Consulate. *(Standing)*

COLONEL: But of course. *(Rising)* Thank you for stopping by, Mr. Kempler.

DAY TWO

COLONEL: Good day, Mr. Kempler.

KEMPLER: I have a letter from my ambassador.

COLONEL: Is that so?

KEMPLER: Please... *(Handing it over)*

COLONEL: It's addressed to myself. And in his hand. *(Pause)* Why didn't he call? *(Pause)* Very well. *(Puts letter down without reading)* What more can I do for you?

KEMPLER: Damn it, you can read the letter.

COLONEL: *(Obliging KEMPLER)* Yes, all right then. *(Pause)* But he makes no mention of venereal disease.

KEMPLER: Venereal disease?

COLONEL: Syphilis, yes.

KEMPLER: You will either release her, or let my doctor see her.

COLONEL: Bring in your doctor, Mr. Kempler.

KEMPLER: I shall.

COLONEL: But I doubt that he will contest our reports.

KEMPLER: I hope this will cost you your rank.

COLONEL: Are you Jewish, Mr. Kempler?

KEMPLER: What?

COLONEL: What is your religion?

KEMPLER: How does that matter?

COLONEL: Not in the slightest. But tell me.

KEMPLER: I've been overseas for fifteen years and have never experienced such idiocy.

COLONEL: I won't let you flatter me, Mr. Kempler.

KEMPLER: Colonel, you are an idiot of some caliber.

COLONEL: We will become better friends in time.

KEMPLER: What do you hope to gain from this?

COLONEL: Perhaps your imagination is running away. I am not a sinister man. Look, here is a picture of my family. *(Shows photo on his desk)* I am hardworking. This office takes the worst abuse. Come now, have a cigarette.

KEMPLER: Why have you abducted my wife?

COLONEL: I have already told you.

KEMPLER: You dressed her and photographed her. It's all very entertaining. Who are you trying to hurt?

COLONEL: No one.

KEMPLER: Her bank has received complaints.

COLONEL: Yes, I have spoken directly with her officers.

KEMPLER: You are committing crimes against Americans.

COLONEL: I happen to like your nation.

KEMPLER: Then why this punishment?

COLONEL: Your wife was fraternizing with our army.

KEMPLER: This is very wrong.

COLONEL: *(Removing a sack from inside his desk)* I have some of her personal things. You may wish to take them with you. *(Opening sack. Handling folded blouse delicately.)* She wears contact lenses. Have you a pair of glasses for her? *(Pause)* Perhaps you can bring them tomorrow.

KEMPLER: Please let me see her for one minute.

COLONEL: And suppose I should let you. What then? You would want her released on the spot. You would raise your voice and get in more difficulties with us. It is better to follow procedures.

KEMPLER: You're detaining an innocent woman.

COLONEL: What is your wish, Mr. Kempler? Do you want her free? Do you want her well? Really, we can straighten this out with remarkable civility.

KEMPLER: I doubt it.

COLONEL: Then what do you suggest? I don't want your wife here. I am embarrassed to see you here. I don't want letters from your embassy. Do you hear me clearly? Do you think we can try, Mr. Kempler?

KEMPLER: I don't know.

COLONEL: You must at least trust me in this matter.

KEMPLER: I'd like to see my wife.

COLONEL: And you will.

KEMPLER: What did she do to warrant this?

COLONEL: Mrs. Kempler was arrested for soliciting on the streets.

KEMPLER: Is it because she works at the bank?

COLONEL: I don't think so.

KEMPLER: You know of course it is an international bank.

COLONEL: Yes.

KEMPLER: It is a powerful bank.

COLONEL: I realize that.

KEMPLER: Is it my work then?

COLONEL: You put yourself in a curious position, Mr. Kempler.

KEMPLER: My company's policies are very liberal here.

COLONEL: What are your company's policies?

KEMPLER: We hire locally. At least two-thirds. Few Algerians.

COLONEL: Are you Jewish, Mr. Kempler?

KEMPLER: Why do you continue on that?

COLONEL: Because I don't like Jews.

KEMPLER: We appreciate these business opportunities in Fez.

COLONEL: Tell me what you are.

KEMPLER: Yes, I am Jewish.

COLONEL: I am not surprised.

KEMPLER: But my wife is not.

COLONEL: I am not an anti-Semite, Mr. Kempler. My opinions are rather mild. *(Pause)* Is your architectural firm from New York?

KEMPLER: Yes.

COLONEL: But the names are not Jewish? *(Pause)* Somehow we're always doing business with Jews.

KEMPLER: We'll build more with time.

COLONEL: You make generous payments under the table to a long list of people. It is an interesting arrangement.

KEMPLER: Why did you stage those photographs?

COLONEL: What?

KEMPLER: They were staged.

COLONEL: Shall we discuss architecture? Are we really in store for American skyscrapers? What beautiful dreams have you waiting for us?

KEMPLER: The designs are very exciting.

COLONEL: Are we making you fat and bored? Why do you architects put bathrooms in the oddest of places? *(Pause)* Don't be silent with me.

KEMPLER: What would you like to hear?

COLONEL: What would I like to hear? Anything you care to say.

KEMPLER: You seem to know enough.

COLONEL: Then you should go back to your hotel and rehearse.

KEMPLER: Rehearse what?

COLONEL: Stories. Make up a story.

KEMPLER: I will.

COLONEL: That's good to hear. *(Pause)* Let us talk tomorrow. Good afternoon.

DAY THREE

COLONEL: I see that you have brought your physician.

KEMPLER: With your permission.

COLONEL: Yes, but of course.

KEMPLER: Is he with her now?

COLONEL: Yes.

KEMPLER: How is she?

COLONEL: Fine.

KEMPLER: Has she slept?

COLONEL: Yes.

KEMPLER: And eating?

COLONEL: I believe so.

KEMPLER: I will see her today.

COLONEL: You will wait.

KEMPLER: I have some of her things.

COLONEL: Leave them with me.

KEMPLER: And her glasses.

COLONEL: Thank you.

KEMPLER: I must have her home.

COLONEL: We will try.

KEMPLER: We are seldom apart.

COLONEL: I sympathize.

KEMPLER: Will there be a formal arraignment?

COLONEL: It has already occurred. *(Pause)* You will receive notice of the trial.

KEMPLER: How soon?

COLONEL: Perhaps in a few weeks.

KEMPLER: Must it go to trial?

COLONEL: I'm afraid so.

KEMPLER: Why is she being set up?

COLONEL: I cannot answer that.

KEMPLER: Our country has good relations with yours.

COLONEL: Yes.

KEMPLER: There must be a way to resolve this.

COLONEL: Return to your consulate, Mr. Kempler.

KEMPLER: Surely you could intervene?

COLONEL: I could not.

KEMPLER: And what if the doctor says that she is fine?

COLONEL: But she is not.

KEMPLER: God help you if you cause her pain.

COLONEL: She is being given penicillin.

KEMPLER: You better not fuck around with her.

COLONEL: Go home and get some sleep.

KEMPLER: I'll wait for the doctor.

COLONEL: Go home, Mr. Kempler.

DAY FOUR

COLONEL: Did you know that we had to devalue our currency?

KEMPLER: I heard this morning.

COLONEL: It is unfortunate. Nothing keeps stable.

KEMPLER: Many countries have the same problem.

COLONEL: Thanks to the London economists, it is cheap to see Morocco.

KEMPLER: Yes, it is.

COLONEL: Now my salary will buy even less groceries for tomorrow. *(Pause)* How are your hotel accommodations?

KEMPLER: Sufficient.

COLONEL: We have remarkably fine hotels.

KEMPLER: Yes, I would agree.

COLONEL: Did your physician report back to you?

KEMPLER: Yes.

COLONEL: He corroborated with our doctors?

KEMPLER: Yes.

COLONEL: It needn't be a mystery.

KEMPLER: My wife is in your jail.

COLONEL: Only temporarily.

KEMPLER: The doctor said it is an early infection.

COLONEL: Yes, we caught it quickly.

KEMPLER: Your medics gave it to her.

COLONEL: No, Mr. Kempler.

KEMPLER: She told my doctor they did.

COLONEL: Out of embarrassment, no doubt.

KEMPLER: You son-of-a-bitch.

COLONEL: Sit down, Mr. Kempler

KEMPLER: Your fucking medics gave it to her.

COLONEL: Why ever should they?

KEMPLER: I demand to see her.

COLONEL: Let me tell you something, my friend. I met your wife on two occasions. She is quite beautiful. I would like to sleep with her myself.

KEMPLER: We should be able to strike a deal.

COLONEL: Not in that tone of voice.

KEMPLER: I don't understand you, Colonel.

COLONEL: Whisper to me, Mr. Kempler.

KEMPLER: Go screw yourself.

COLONEL: You're not whispering.

KEMPLER: There's a limit to this business.

COLONEL: Why don't you contact Amnesty International?

KEMPLER: I have.

COLONEL: And the Red Cross.

KEMPLER: I have.

COLONEL: And your ambassador calls me every day.

KEMPLER: I know why you're doing this.

COLONEL: Tell me, Mr. Kempler.

KEMPLER: You're crazy.

COLONEL: Yes.

KEMPLER: Very crazy.

COLONEL: It's become a sporting thing.

KEMPLER: You find some prosperous Americans...

COLONEL: Please go on.

KEMPLER: And you play with their lives.

COLONEL: I am an officer in the King's army.

KEMPLER: How did you ever get to be Colonel?

COLONEL: I speak English.

KEMPLER: You are causing me great inconvenience.

COLONEL: That's putting it mildly. Why be so kind?

KEMPLER: Then you admit it.

COLONEL: Admit what?

KEMPLER: What you're doing to my wife.

COLONEL: Your wife is very well educated.

KEMPLER: What is that supposed to mean?

COLONEL: Our women are hardly schooled.

KEMPLER: Are you punishing her for that?

COLONEL: No.

KEMPLER: Then why bring it up?

COLONEL: My wife stays home with our children.

KEMPLER: Your nation is very backward.

COLONEL: My nation is based on tradition.

KEMPLER: Your people are illiterate.

COLONEL: I cannot argue that.

KEMPLER: But why snap at my wife?

COLONEL: Mr. Kempler, I told you. I like your wife. *(Silence)* Tomorrow you may see her.

DAY FIVE

COLONEL: You are the first person I see each day.

KEMPLER: The privilege is mutual.

COLONEL: Did I make a promise to you?

KEMPLER: I believe so.

COLONEL: Then I won't keep you any further.

KEMPLER: Thank you.

COLONEL: You needn't thank me. *(Pause)* I see you decided to shave. *(Pause)* You look very presentable. *(Picks lint from* KEMPLER's *jacket)*

KEMPLER: How much time do I get?

COLONEL: As long as you want. *(Pause)* Go right ahead, Mr. Kempler.

*(*KEMPLER *hesitates with his exit. Some fear over meeting his wife.)*

DAY SIX

COLONEL: How good to see you, Mr. Kempler. *(Pause)* We have the trial date.

KEMPLER: When?

COLONEL: Three weeks.

KEMPLER: Why so long?

COLONEL: It is the best we can do.

KEMPLER: What about bail?

COLONEL: No, I'm sorry.

KEMPLER: My ambassador says there is no precedent for this detention.

COLONEL: Well, I think we shall work around it.

KEMPLER: My wife needs to see a dentist.

COLONEL: Did she request that?

KEMPLER: Yes.

COLONEL: All right then.

KEMPLER: She would like unsoiled clothes.

COLONEL: The wash is done weekly.

KEMPLER: I would like to give her some reading material.

COLONEL: She has magazines in her quarters.

KEMPLER: Please make her feel comfortable.

COLONEL: Yes, Mr. Kempler.

KEMPLER: There are insects in her bed. *(Pause)* I would appreciate anything you can do.

COLONEL: Of course. She will get another bed.

KEMPLER: And paper for the lavatory.

COLONEL: Certainly.

KEMPLER: My ambassador will be stopping by sometime today.

COLONEL: Thank you for telling me.

KEMPLER: And an American journalist.

COLONEL: Fine.

KEMPLER: How long will this go on?

COLONEL: Be patient if you can.

KEMPLER: It is wrong.

COLONEL: How are things at the Industrial Park?

KEMPLER: All right.

COLONEL: On schedule?

KEMPLER: Yes.

COLONEL: Do you walk around with a little lunch pail?

KEMPLER: I do.

COLONEL: Sit, Mr. Kempler. Today let's make it a social visit.

KEMPLER: No, thank you.

COLONEL: When was the last time you slept with Mrs. Kempler?

KEMPLER: Go to hell.

COLONEL: I'm only suggesting your good health.

KEMPLER: I've been examined.

COLONEL: That was prudent.

KEMPLER: No, my attorney suggested it.

COLONEL: Then you will appear in court.

KEMPLER: If need be.

COLONEL: The men in my command will support these charges quite graphically.

KEMPLER: Of course.

COLONEL: Take me seriously.

KEMPLER: Army life must suit you.

COLONEL: It is respectable.

KEMPLER: The stench permeates the uniform.

COLONEL: It is the king's army.

KEMPLER: How many women do you have locked away?

COLONEL: Not as many as Iran.

KEMPLER: But quite a bit.

COLONEL: A fair share.

KEMPLER: For solicitation?

COLONEL: In many instances.

KEMPLER: Do the convictions hold?

COLONEL: Ask your attorney.

KEMPLER: I'm asking you.

COLONEL: They hold.

KEMPLER: She's willing to leave the country.

COLONEL: Invariably.

KEMPLER: She's not like other women.

COLONEL: I hope not.

KEMPLER: They live on the streets.

COLONEL: There's a reflex in Moroccan life which attempts what I like to call human betterment. Penal life is part of that reflex.

KEMPLER: You don't care about these women.

COLONEL: But I do. I am a humanitarian.

KEMPLER: You are a racist, Colonel.

COLONEL: Am I?

KEMPLER: You know what I mean.

COLONEL: We are all children of Abraham.

KEMPLER: I think not.

COLONEL: One would like to believe it. *(Pause)* How do you reconcile yourself, Mr. Kempler, spending your talents in the Arab world?

KEMPLER: I don't have to.

COLONEL: Certainly you have principles.

KEMPLER: Thank you for your time. *(About to leave)*

COLONEL: Your wife is of Arab descent, Mr. Kempler. Did you know that?

DAY SEVEN

COLONEL: There will be a dentist coming this afternoon.

KEMPLER: How is she today?

COLONEL: In good spirits.

KEMPLER: Is she in a private cell?

COLONEL: Yes.

KEMPLER: My ambassador said there will be some developments in the next few hours.

COLONEL: Did he say that?

KEMPLER: Yes.

COLONEL: He seems to be very influential in our city.

KEMPLER: It would be a good thing.

COLONEL: The ambassador is a close acquaintance of the commissioner.

KEMPLER: Is that a fact?

COLONEL: You have used your leverage, Mr. Kempler.

KEMPLER: She's had enough of your hospitality.

COLONEL: And you're getting to be a nuisance. *(Pause)* There are some women here waiting for several years.

KEMPLER: I'm tired of waiting.

COLONEL: Go listen to some music. Leave, please.

KEMPLER: You will hear more from us.

COLONEL: A paperback about Morocco?

KEMPLER: You know, every dirty restaurant has a bit of you inside it. I see many men with your face.

COLONEL: Perhaps you ought to see a doctor.

KEMPLER: I'd like to see my wife now.

COLONEL: Yes, go right ahead.

KEMPLER: Thank you.

COLONEL: Today your wife confessed.

KEMPLER: Confessed?

COLONEL: To the charges.

KEMPLER: Why should she?

COLONEL: Because she is guilty.

KEMPLER: This is terribly wrong.

COLONEL: Would you like me to read her affidavit?

KEMPLER: No.

COLONEL: It's very short.

KEMPLER: I can imagine how you worded it.

COLONEL: Yes, well...I'll leave a copy with you. (KEMPLER *reads and is quietly devastated.)* This should expedite things.

KEMPLER: Did you bargain with her?

COLONEL: Why don't you ask your wife?

KEMPLER: I will.

COLONEL: And ask her if she was treated with respect.

KEMPLER: *(Pocketing affidavit)* Any other matter to settle?

COLONEL: You can see your wife now.

KEMPLER: Fine.

COLONEL: How is your building project?

KEMPLER: Why do you ask?

COLONEL: When is ribbon-cutting?

KEMPLER: Fairly soon.

COLONEL: Please do invite me.

KEMPLER: You are on my list.

COLONEL: How thoughtful.

KEMPLER: Aren't you ever given a day off?

COLONEL: It's a ten-day shift.

KEMPLER: You could stand a change of clothes.

COLONEL: Yes, forgive me.

KEMPLER: It's quite all right.

COLONEL: My wife is to blame. *(Pause)* She works very hard, Mr. Kempler.

KEMPLER: Perhaps we could get together some afternoon for tea?

COLONEL: A very kind suggestion.

KEMPLER: Then after Abril is released.

COLONEL: If luck so has it.

KEMPLER: For a moment you can pretend that I'm not a Jew.

COLONEL: For a moment.

DAY EIGHT

KEMPLER: Renovation?

COLONEL: They're bringing indoor plumbing into the dormitories.

KEMPLER: It's a nice touch to the facility.

COLONEL: Yes, we think so.

KEMPLER: My country is beginning extradition proceedings. A change of venue.

COLONEL: God's speed to you.

KEMPLER: Her confession is void.

COLONEL: Is it?

KEMPLER: She copied it from your steno.

COLONEL: It is in plain English, and in her hand.

KEMPLER: She had no choice. *(Pause)* I hope you will stop annoying her with your impromptu visits. She's not starved for conversation.

COLONEL: A jailer must look after his guests. To lessen the loneliness of these long days. Am I not a bright conversationalist? I watch your wife through her prison window, I tap the door several times, I hand her a cigarette and a sweet pastry. Can you take issue with me on this? *(Noticing* KEMPLER's *disdain)* You exasperate me, Mr. Kempler.

KEMPLER: I expect these incidents to end without further pain.

COLONEL: You will get your wish.

KEMPLER: I speak for my wife as you know.

COLONEL: You are a hero in my eyes. A cigarette?

KEMPLER: This time next week we will be in New York.

COLONEL: Be careful with us.

KEMPLER: Our memories of Fez will fall into the nearest sewer.

COLONEL: Her looseness is no reflection on my city.

KEMPLER: It is fiction.

COLONEL: Be careful that Mrs. Kempler does not repeat herself in some other town.

KEMPLER: I don't think so. *(Pause)* I wish my country could extend to you the same hospitality you have shown to us.

COLONEL: That would be welcoming. We are both Semitic, in a manner of speaking.

KEMPLER: I wouldn't be cheerful about it.

COLONEL: Why not?

KEMPLER: Because it is a depressing picture.

COLONEL: Only if you think so.

KEMPLER: Your people have so many resources.

COLONEL: Your people too.

KEMPLER: But I'm talking about your natural resources, your lands.

COLONEL: You may build for us. I think that is fair.

KEMPLER: It isn't.

COLONEL: But it is American. Labor for contract.

KEMPLER: With good will.

COLONEL: If there is any...

KEMPLER: Someone ought to build a real facility instead of keeping this stable.

COLONEL: Why not bid for it?

KEMPLER: Next year.

COLONEL: Yes, when you visit us next year. *(Pause)* You and I make conversation easily.

KEMPLER: It is marvelous, Colonel.

COLONEL: I never know when you're joking, Mr. Kempler.

DAY NINE

COLONEL: Sit down, Mr. Kempler. I have the recent medic's report. *(Pause)* Her treatment is going accordingly and should cure her totally. No allergic reaction from the patient. Eating habits are normal. Her blood pressure is good. The dental work begun earlier in the week has been completed. Apparently they built a cap around one of the teeth. And that is our report. *(Pause)* Any questions?

KEMPLER: No.

COLONEL: Good.

KEMPLER: She'll be leaving tomorrow?

COLONEL: Luck is on your side.

KEMPLER: It is too long.

COLONEL: Think, in a few hours this will be over and you and your wife will be together.

KEMPLER: You're right.

COLONEL: You don't look happy, Mr. Kempler.

KEMPLER: I am very happy.

COLONEL: How about smiling a little?

KEMPLER: I am smiling.

COLONEL: Let's have a celebration drink. *(Brings out bottle from desk)* These times are brief.

KEMPLER: Just a short one, thanks.

COLONEL: L'chaim.

KEMPLER: Same to you.

(They drink.)

COLONEL: Another?

KEMPLER: No.

COLONEL: Must you hate me every morning?

KEMPLER: Yes.

COLONEL: *(Pours himself a second drink)* You would like to cheat me?

KEMPLER: How could I cheat you?

COLONEL: You make more money than I. You dress well. You have a very exciting wife. You travel around the world.

KEMPLER: And you can rot in your jail.

COLONEL: Yes, exactly. I can rot in my jail.

KEMPLER: You elicit sympathy, Colonel.

COLONEL: Yes, I know. *(Laughing)* It's a jail full of fugitive women. Half of them were found on their back. I am their warden. I am their shepherd. *(Pause)* They have sad lives. You can understand.

KEMPLER: I'd like to see my wife now.

COLONEL: Let her wait a moment. *(Pause)* You won't be allowed physical contact with her for some time. You must be patient with her problem.

KEMPLER: Thank you for the advice.

COLONEL: You may hug her all you want.

KEMPLER: Thanks.

COLONEL: Kissing is at your discretion. *(Pause)* Have you any children?

KEMPLER: No.

COLONEL: I have six. My oldest is fourteen. He has my features. My son is very important to me. He has a temper like the devil.

KEMPLER: We wish your family well.

COLONEL: Do you plan to have a family?

KEMPLER: Perhaps.

COLONEL: Do you like baseball, Mr. Kempler?

KEMPLER: Not too much.

COLONEL: It is a popular thing?

KEMPLER: Yes.

COLONEL: We have races here.

KEMPLER: What sort of races?

COLONEL: Dog races.

KEMPLER: I thought this was a religious city.

COLONEL: Would you like to join me for a race?

KEMPLER: What do you expect me to say?

COLONEL: Why do you always answer me with another question?

KEMPLER: I'd rather you show me a few of your mosques.

COLONEL: Unfortunately that is not permitted.

KEMPLER: I've seen the one in Meknes.

COLONEL: You must be Moslem to see the mosques.

KEMPLER: Why not arrange something for me?

COLONEL: Would you like an armband with a yellow star?

KEMPLER: No.

COLONEL: Why did you marry a Gentile?

KEMPLER: I have no answer.

COLONEL: Aren't you religious, Mr. Kempler? I'm told that you are.

KEMPLER: No.

COLONEL: You get strident like a foolish zealot.

KEMPLER: No, not at all.

COLONEL: Have I created a zealot then?

KEMPLER: No.

COLONEL: Is it good to be a Jew?

KEMPLER: It is.

COLONEL: I can only wonder, Mr. Kempler. *(Pause)* You seem to tell me so little. *(Pause)* Is this secrecy Jewish?

DAY TEN

COLONEL: Good day, Mr. Kempler. *(Long silence)* Your wife is waiting for you in the next room.

END OF ACT ONE

ACT TWO

(Some days later. Evening. An expensive restaurant in Malaga, Spain. Tables on the terrace. Lights rise. Perhaps there is Spanish guitar music. KEMPLER is downstage, lighting a cigarette. He sees MRS. KEMPLER entering. He joins her, smiles. A silence.)

KEMPLER: You were gone a long time.

MRS. KEMPLER: I couldn't find the lavatory.

KEMPLER: I've ordered for you. *(Pause)* Clams.

MRS. KEMPLER: Excellent.

KEMPLER: Salad. Local wine.

MRS. KEMPLER: And you?

KEMPLER: Chateaubriand.

MRS. KEMPLER: Is Ralph coming?

KEMPLER: No.

MRS. KEMPLER: Really?

KEMPLER: He cancelled.

MRS. KEMPLER: That's strange.

KEMPLER: He's under the weather. Left word with the hotel desk.

MRS. KEMPLER: I'm disappointed.

KEMPLER: So am I, darling.

MRS. KEMPLER: Then shall we phone him afterwards?

KEMPLER: If you like.

MRS. KEMPLER: Is it cool out here?

KEMPLER: Yes, take my jacket.

MRS. KEMPLER: No, darling. I'll be all right.

KEMPLER: A cocktail?

MRS. KEMPLER: No, I think not. What are you drinking?

KEMPLER: Vodka.

MRS. KEMPLER: May I? *(Sipping)* How long are we going to stay?

KEMPLER: At the hotel?

MRS. KEMPLER: It's a lovely hotel. The austere view of the harbor and the Plaza Del Toros. I love Spain in September, don't you?

KEMPLER: We'll stay a few more days. It's up to you.

MRS. KEMPLER: Won't you need to get back this week?

KEMPLER: No, I made arrangements.

MRS. KEMPLER: Still...

KEMPLER: Don't worry your little head.

MRS. KEMPLER: I know your deadline, Charles.

(A WAITER enters, serves KEMPLER and MRS. KEMPLER wine, exits. They hold up their glasses.)

KEMPLER: Shall we toast?

MRS. KEMPLER: What will it be tonight?

KEMPLER: To good living.

MRS. KEMPLER: Cheers.

(They touch glasses, drink.)

MRS. KEMPLER: I'm having the worst difficulty with my makeup this evening. Does it show?

KEMPLER: No, no.

MRS. KEMPLER: But my mascara, Charles?

KEMPLER: Perhaps it's perspiration.

MRS. KEMPLER: Not so loud.

KEMPLER: Aren't you feeling well?

MRS. KEMPLER: Yes, I think so.

KEMPLER: Are you having chills?

MRS. KEMPLER: Earlier. I'm fine now.

KEMPLER: We can stay in tonight.

MRS. KEMPLER: Let's see, darling.

KEMPLER: Am I doting over you?

MRS. KEMPLER: Of course not.

(They hold hands briefly.)

KEMPLER: It becomes second nature for me.

MRS. KEMPLER: A model husband you are.

KEMPLER: An inept model.

MRS. KEMPLER: Are you fishing for sympathy?

KEMPLER: *(Playful)* Yes.

MRS. KEMPLER: You can have anything from me, but sympathy.

KEMPLER: You're looking healthier, Mrs. Kempler.

MRS. KEMPLER: It's the wine.

KEMPLER: What would you like to do tomorrow?

MRS. KEMPLER: The gardens at the Alcazaba?

KEMPLER: And afterwards?

MRS. KEMPLER: Let's picnic and get drunk silly.

KEMPLER: I see you're feeling back in stride.

MRS. KEMPLER: Some have jet lag. Perhaps it was jail lag. *(Touching her tooth)*

KEMPLER: The cap again?

MRS. KEMPLER: The dental work was done by a gorilla.

KEMPLER: We could always have the work checked. *(Pause)* At least they didn't charge for it.

MRS. KEMPLER: Oh, but they did.

KEMPLER: One cannot sue a foreign government.

MRS. KEMPLER: Not if I could have my way.

KEMPLER: We'll put this behind us. A great story to tell our friends in the States. One day we'll have a good laugh over it. *(Pause)* They were getting to me through you.

MRS. KEMPLER: Why?

KEMPLER: I had no business being there.

MRS. KEMPLER: Darling, nothing was illegal.

KEMPLER: They knew my firm was Jewish, fronting through affiliates.

MRS. KEMPLER: Morocco is not Syria, Charles.

KEMPLER: Every Arab nation plays games.

MRS. KEMPLER: True.

KEMPLER: Are you upset with me?

MRS. KEMPLER: No.

KEMPLER: I did everything humanly possible.

MRS. KEMPLER: Perhaps had you offered cash, instead of a check...

KEMPLER: The banks were closed.

MRS. KEMPLER: Or your Rolex...

KEMPLER: Perhaps. Who's to say? Perhaps I was too aggressive? I thought I did my best. *(Pause)* Where is the waiter?

MRS. KEMPLER: It's a three-star kitchen, Charles. When they're ready.

KEMPLER: We should have ordered in. Did you hear about your transfer?

MRS. KEMPLER: Not yet.

KEMPLER: Will it be any problem?

MRS. KEMPLER: Hardly.

KEMPLER: What's your preference? You needn't work everything around me.

MRS. KEMPLER: Whatever darling.

KEMPLER: We can stay in Europe.

MRS. KEMPLER: Fine.

KEMPLER: Or Japan.

MRS. KEMPLER: I really don't care.

KEMPLER: Well, I'd just as soon stay in the Mediterrean.

MRS. KEMPLER: One telegram would suffice.

KEMPLER: You do have more flexibility.

MRS. KEMPLER: We just have to buy some more summer clothes.

KEMPLER: A more conservative look.

MRS. KEMPLER: Fashion first.

KEMPLER: Leave cleavage to the ladies in Vegas.

MRS. KEMPLER: And what about my umbrage?

KEMPLER: I'm so hungry this evening.

MRS. KEMPLER: Have another drink.

KEMPLER: Why do you encourage me?

MRS. KEMPLER: Because you're different when you drink.

KEMPLER: Different than what?

MRS. KEMPLER: Different than sober.

KEMPLER: Why can't I be sober?

MRS. KEMPLER: We're on holiday...

(WAITER *enters, serves appetizers.* KEMPLER *and* MRS. KEMPLER *sit at table.)*

KEMPLER: It's peculiar how Arabs drink everywhere but in public sight. Hemp in their cigarettes. Their hidden nightclubs...

MRS. KEMPLER: It's a veiled society. They mask vice artfully.

KEMPLER: And they know how to protect their women.

MRS. KEMPLER: Yes, like beloved livestock. I don't want to discuss the inanities of the Arab world.

KEMPLER: The wisdom of inanities.

MRS. KEMPLER: To find women displaced under the peasants, who are under the merchants and militia, who are under the politically affluent...makes me very ashamed of my background. This casual degradation has become all too embarrassing, particularly when it hits home, Charles.

KEMPLER: I thought you were immune to it.

MRS. KEMPLER: If only I were...

KEMPLER: I'll never forget his odor.

MRS. KEMPLER: The Colonel?

KEMPLER: His wonderfully cheap tobacco and dank-mold carpets. He knew I found him abhorrent. For his dirtiness, above all.

MRS. KEMPLER: Yes, darling, you see...cleanliness is looked upon as a very alien characteristic. Grounds for suspicion and deportation. Unless one is very religious.

KEMPLER: They all say they're religious.

MRS. KEMPLER: Even peasants want respect.

KEMPLER: He was a peasant.

MRS. KEMPLER: For a peasant, he spoke excellent English. (Pause) I really believed he liked you, Charles.

KEMPLER: Liked me?

MRS. KEMPLER: He spoke highly of you. Admired your suits. Enjoyed your humor. Oh, he was a little crazy. You can understand that. How often does a jailor catch an American? When he talked to me in Arabic, he forgot his rank. You didn't cause him offense.

KEMPLER: He told you so?

MRS. KEMPLER: Yes.

KEMPLER: What else did he tell you?

MRS. KEMPLER: Very little else.

KEMPLER: They've kept the photographs.

MRS. KEMPLER: I really don't know.

KEMPLER: How many were there?

MRS. KEMPLER: Men? I thought we weren't going to discuss this another time.

KEMPLER: Everything you told me in jail was contradictory.

MRS. KEMPLER: I had a terrible fever then.

KEMPLER: Why do you bring up inconsistencies?

MRS. KEMPLER: Talk to my doctor, Charles.

KEMPLER: I have talked with him.

MRS. KEMPLER: Wonderful.

KEMPLER: What am I to think?

MRS. KEMPLER: Think what you want. Thank God I survived Morocco.

KEMPLER: I have thanked God.

MRS. KEMPLER: I wish I could believe you.

KEMPLER: I have thanked God.

MRS. KEMPLER: I know exactly what you went through.

KEMPLER: Do you?

MRS. KEMPLER: I do.

KEMPLER: Doubts don't comfort me.

MRS. KEMPLER: I don't sleep around. You think I do.

KEMPLER: That's not the issue.

MRS. KEMPLER: What is the issue?

KEMPLER: I don't know, Abril.

MRS. KEMPLER: Charles... *(He looks at her keenly.)* Our marriage is very strong. To hell with everything else. You must believe that. *(Pause)* The photographs continue to bother you.

KEMPLER: Yes.

MRS. KEMPLER: You know what choice they gave me.

KEMPLER: What choice did they give you?

MRS. KEMPLER: *(Dryly)* Use your imagination.

KEMPLER: I'd rather not.

MRS. KEMPLER: I was harassed on the street by their soldiers. It was nothing more than that. I was alone. One of their soldiers mistook me for something I wasn't. Everything was contrived to protect him. A little fiction goes a long way in Fez.

KEMPLER: You don't have to defend yourself.

MRS. KEMPLER: Thank you.

KEMPLER: Everything was divisive.

MRS. KEMPLER: Perhaps that was the point.

KEMPLER: Why were you at the bar?

MRS. KEMPLER: Drinking, of course.

KEMPLER: Couldn't you have waited for a girlfriend?

MRS. KEMPLER: I was working late that evening. And so were you.

KEMPLER: Why did you provoke the soldiers?

MRS. KEMPLER: I don't like being followed into the Medina.

KEMPLER: In Morocco you told me a different story.

MRS. KEMPLER: Did I?

KEMPLER: You said the incident started at the bank office.

MRS. KEMPLER: I was targeted, Charles. Leave it at that.

KEMPLER: I'd like a better explanation.

MRS. KEMPLER: Do I take an oath before answering?

KEMPLER: Please.

MRS. KEMPLER: Sleep with cockroaches for a month, then ask me any question you want.

KEMPLER: Don't make a game of it.

MRS. KEMPLER: It was not a game, Charles.

KEMPLER: The photographs don't show an inhibited woman.

MRS. KEMPLER: What do they show?

KEMPLER: An unforgettable licentiousness.

MRS. KEMPLER: *(Rising from table in anger)* You can't say that, Charles. I can't bear the hurt.

KEMPLER: Did they drug you? Why was it so difficult to see you?

MRS. KEMPLER: You know the jails. Maybe I was unconscious. I was in a state of fright. *(Pause)* Do you think you married a prostitute?

KEMPLER: Don't be absurd.

MRS. KEMPLER: Does it give you a vicarious thrill?

KEMPLER: Abril!

MRS. KEMPLER: It's true, Charles. We seem to feed each other's lurid fantasies.

KEMPLER: I don't like punishment.

MRS. KEMPLER: Nor do I. These last few days, I feel like a stranger to myself. *(Pause)* Why are you staring at me?

KEMPLER: I'm not the one to comment on moral conduct.

MRS. KEMPLER: Why don't you?

KEMPLER: Because I'm more caught up on your motives.

MRS. KEMPLER: My motives?

KEMPLER: Your hedonism. Your exhibitionism and contempt for social rules. You'll always be promiscuous. Since the first day I've known you.

MRS. KEMPLER: I did not sleep with the Moroccan army. Even at gunpoint.

KEMPLER: Then my thinking is very twisted.

MRS. KEMPLER: Obviously.

KEMPLER: Give me a sign, Abril, something to hold on to.

MRS. KEMPLER: No vaccine in the world could withstand a Moroccan soldier. No vaccine could immune you from your worst fears. We can only make do with what we now have. I love you, Charles. Think of the bright side. They were very considerate. We can have relations again.

KEMPLER: Yes, it's remarkably accommodating of them. *(Spills drink)* Damn it!

MRS. KEMPLER: Have another then.

KEMPLER: It's just as well.

MRS. KEMPLER: You believe I was whoring.

KEMPLER: Yes, I do.

MRS. KEMPLER: To what purpose?

KEMPLER: Kicks.

MRS. KEMPLER: Like taking drugs?

KEMPLER: Like fucking soldiers.

MRS. KEMPLER: That's enough! *(Getting her composure)* My breeding's better than yours. I was at Oxford, darling.

KEMPLER: You're part Arab.

MRS. KEMPLER: We're supreme racehorses and mythmakers.

KEMPLER: I tip my hat to you.

MRS. KEMPLER: And I'm part Spanish. A double import. From both sides of the Mediterranean.

KEMPLER: A sterling combination.

MRS. KEMPLER: How long do you intend to chaff?

KEMPLER: How long do you intend to embarrass us?

MRS. KEMPLER: Indefinitely.

KEMPLER: Wonderful.

MRS. KEMPLER: What sort of guarantee are you looking for?

KEMPLER: Fidelity being outside your vocabulary, any guarantee could only extend ninety days at best.

MRS. KEMPLER: You don't know the limit of my vocabulary. You don't know my capacity for change. You're really not being fair to me. You don't know the pain I feel.

KEMPLER: I do.

MRS. KEMPLER: Then why these doubts?

KEMPLER: You were on good terms with the Colonel.

MRS. KEMPLER: I needed an ally in that hovel.

KEMPLER: Do you know what the ambassador asked me?

MRS. KEMPLER: Yes, you told me.

KEMPLER: "Mr. Kempler, wives overseas often need mad money. Does your wife indulge herself after hours?" *(Pause)* "Mr. Kempler, your wife is most...charming." *(Pause)* "Mr. Kempler, do you think you can keep an eye on her for the weeks ahead?"

(WAITER enters with entrees.)

MRS. KEMPLER: Are you looking for a moral, Charles? What exactly is the point?

(WAITER leaves, after catching a fleeting glance from her.)

KEMPLER: If we lived in a small town, gossip would dampen your spirits.

MRS. KEMPLER: I don't like small towns.

KEMPLER: So we wander like globetrotters.

MRS. KEMPLER: Haven't you had an affair in the last year or two?

KEMPLER: *(Perhaps a lie)* No.

MRS. KEMPLER: You wouldn't tell me anyway.

KEMPLER: You'd know the moment I do. I can't lie.

MRS. KEMPLER: Oh, you lie famously.

KEMPLER: Not to you.

MRS. KEMPLER: How would I know?

KEMPLER: Because you're more skillful at it.

MRS. KEMPLER: Are we going to dine, or argue?

KEMPLER: I have no appetite. You've made me a laughingstock.

MRS. KEMPLER: No one is laughing at you.

KEMPLER: *(Painfully)* They are laughing at me.

MRS. KEMPLER: *(Tenderly, touching his hand)* Charles...

KEMPLER: *(After a pause, softly)* I'm so very much in love with you.

MRS. KEMPLER: Keep telling me that.

KEMPLER: You can be so beautiful.

MRS. KEMPLER: And so can you. I will behave better, darling.

KEMPLER: With each promise, there is a false star overhead.

MRS. KEMPLER: Are you now counting stars?

KEMPLER: I am.

MRS. KEMPLER: *(Coyly)* Count sheep, Charles. You were once extremely romantic.

KEMPLER: In the Peace Corps.

MRS. KEMPLER: Not that many years ago.

KEMPLER: Before I started greying.

MRS. KEMPLER: Success has affected you, darling.

KEMPLER: Why do you say that?

MRS. KEMPLER: There was a time when you gave me special attention.

KEMPLER: Fatigue is a very human thing.

MRS. KEMPLER: Is it really fatigue? *(Pause)* I can't have children. You know that pains me.

KEMPLER: As well as me.

MRS. KEMPLER: Perhaps it's harder for the woman. We can go to all the expensive doctors in the world. It won't remedy the situation.

KEMPLER: Wanting children can be an act of will.

MRS. KEMPLER: Which puts the onus on me.

KEMPLER: No.

MRS. KEMPLER: I knew all my life that I would be childless. Since I was a little girl. I knew I would be refused customary things others are granted. I was marked early. Should I cry about it? Isn't it better that we just spend money on ourselves?

KEMPLER: We don't need money.

MRS. KEMPLER: What a pity not to be broke and hungry, without a prayer in all hell. *(Pause. Kicking off her shoes.)* My head is full of nonsense. Charles, are you going to make love to me tonight?

KEMPLER: Do I need a reservation?

MRS. KEMPLER: *(Laughing)* Oh, yes.

KEMPLER: Is there a room assignment?

MRS. KEMPLER: You know the room.

KEMPLER: Did you speak to the Colonel like that? *(Seeing his wife flustered)* Did you fall in love with him?

MRS. KEMPLER: Charles, piss on your obsessions. *(Pause)* I think we ought to establish some rules between us. Either we are on holiday, or revisiting JUDGMENT AT NUREMBERG.

KEMPLER: We are on holiday. *(He makes a conciliatory gesture.)*

MRS. KEMPLER: Glory be to Heaven.

KEMPLER: Yes, glory be to Heaven. Have we failed each other?

MRS. KEMPLER: No worse than other couples.

KEMPLER: I've lost the gift of forgiveness.

MRS. KEMPLER: Under the circumstances, I can understand. Let's elope again. Let's lose ourselves, Charles. Let's re-invent ourselves. Let's fall in love with our better parts.

KEMPLER: You're sincere.

MRS. KEMPLER: I am.

KEMPLER: Nothing in my life prepared me for you, Abril.

MRS. KEMPLER: As it should be.

KEMPLER: *(Suddenly amused)* I told Ralph.

MRS. KEMPLER: You told Ralph what?

KEMPLER: About the arrest.

MRS. KEMPLER: He must have had a good laugh.

KEMPLER: He did.

MRS. KEMPLER: Wasn't Ralph's wife arrested?

KEMPLER: Yes, cocaine.

MRS. KEMPLER: You and Ralph ought to start a club.

KEMPLER: We're working on it.

MRS. KEMPLER: Do you want a divorce, Charles?

KEMPLER: No.

MRS. KEMPLER: Are you certain?

KEMPLER: I'm in love with you.

MRS. KEMPLER: Do you think I'm schizophrenic?

KEMPLER: Yes.

MRS. KEMPLER: My problem is not hopeless.

KEMPLER: I could always rent you out to parties.

MRS. KEMPLER: Charles, are you in a good mood today?

KEMPLER: Yes, I think so.

MRS. KEMPLER: That's good. When you're in a good mood, I'm in a good mood.

KEMPLER: Then we should leave right now.

MRS. KEMPLER: I haven't touched my plate.

KEMPLER: We should pack and fly out tonight.

MRS. KEMPLER: Leave Spain?

KEMPLER: Damn it, let's buy a house in Massachusetts.

MRS. KEMPLER: That is so dull, Charles.

KEMPLER: You owe me this.

MRS. KEMPLER: There are limits.

KEMPLER: Why the hell do we have to live like gypsies?

MRS. KEMPLER: Because I'm part gypsy.

KEMPLER: You're a little of everything. Your father warned me about spending twelve consecutive months with you. You had him around your finger, too. After our wedding, he sent a letter covered with his tears. What did he know, that I don't.

MRS. KEMPLER: (*Avoiding argument*) I really wish Ralph were here tonight. He would arbitrate for us. Every couple needs an arbitrator.

KEMPLER: Shall we ask the waiter?

MRS. KEMPLER: Do what you want darling.

KEMPLER: How do they let you stay on at the bank?

MRS. KEMPLER: I'm very good there.

KEMPLER: But they're reserved people.

MRS. KEMPLER: And so am I.

KEMPLER: And the pope is Jewish.

MRS. KEMPLER: Is he, Charles? I never know when you're joking. *(Pause)* Are we candidates for therapy?

KEMPLER: Exemplary candidates.

MRS. KEMPLER: I'm willing, if you are.

KEMPLER: You would end up sleeping with the psychiatrist.

MRS. KEMPLER: Darling, are we a vaudeville?

KEMPLER: It seems so. Have you slept with Ralph?

MRS. KEMPLER: Why do you ask that?

KEMPLER: Sixth sense.

MRS. KEMPLER: I find it insulting.

KEMPLER: Answer me. Abril...

MRS. KEMPLER: *(Ambiguously)* Once.

KEMPLER: Is that all?

MRS. KEMPLER: Yes, I believe so.

KEMPLER: *(Slow burn)* Then what am I getting all worked up about?

MRS. KEMPLER: I've no idea.

KEMPLER: I feel murderous.

MRS. KEMPLER: Take up golf, darling.

KEMPLER: Why don't you get out your appointment calendar and tell me the nights you're free.

MRS. KEMPLER: Be a sport, Charles. You know my sense of humor.

KEMPLER: You make me cry inside.

MRS. KEMPLER: You're very touching when you cry.

KEMPLER: Do you pity me?

MRS. KEMPLER: Whatever for?

KEMPLER: For my masochism.

MRS. KEMPLER: You?

KEMPLER: Me.

MRS. KEMPLER: No, I don't pity you.

KEMPLER: Do you ever admire me?

MRS. KEMPLER: At certain moments, yes. When you drive with the top down. When you toss your anxieties to the wind.

KEMPLER: Are we competing with each other?

MRS. KEMPLER: These are too many questions for one night. Have another drink. For me?

KEMPLER: There was a time in my life when I had tremendous discipline. Do you remember?

MRS. KEMPLER: Are you over the hill now?

KEMPLER: It occurred to me.

MRS. KEMPLER: Can I tell you the truth, Charles? *(Pause)* You are no longer modern.

KEMPLER: What is that supposed to mean?

MRS. KEMPLER: I think you're closer to the last century. A Victorian caught in the wrong period. You want me to say cruel things. I can be no crueler than this. Strange, that an architect driven by innovation lives with those from the distant past. You are a bit of a relic. An antique. A very vulnerable heart.

KEMPLER: You're just as vulnerable.

MRS. KEMPLER: In some ways.

KEMPLER: I can bruise you.

MRS. KEMPLER: Yes, you could.

KEMPLER: Yet, I'm no harsher than you. Why must we hurt each other so?

MRS. KEMPLER: I don't know, darling. Such things are never simple.

KEMPLER: Your time in jail has softened you. You seem to have acquired something useful.

MRS. KEMPLER: Have I? *(They kiss slowly, passionately.)*

KEMPLER: *(After a pause)* God knows how much I love you.

MRS. KEMPLER: And I...you. Let Morocco fade away. Or we'll go absolutely mad.

KEMPLER: I'll return in a few days.

MRS. KEMPLER: But Charles...

KEMPLER: The complex is planned to open shortly. You understand.

MRS. KEMPLER: We can both go back.

KEMPLER: You remember what the State Department said.

MRS. KEMPLER: Yes, well, if that is what you want.

KEMPLER: Our luck has been perverse all year. *(Pause)* Call Ralph for me.

MRS. KEMPLER: And say what?

KEMPLER: That I'll be out of town.

MRS. KEMPLER: Are you being provocative?

KEMPLER: No.

MRS. KEMPLER: You view Ralph as a rival.

KEMPLER: Not at all.

MRS. KEMPLER: I know you better.

KEMPLER: Call Ralph and say that I know more than I should.

MRS. KEMPLER: But why?

KEMPLER: Let's save our marriage as though our lives were at stake.

MRS. KEMPLER: As you wish.

KEMPLER: I can't do it alone.

MRS. KEMPLER: No one is expecting you to.

KEMPLER: You're so exceptionally bright and gifted, dearest. At times the loveliest woman in creation. I can't fault you for certain excesses, and who am I to make rules for a spirit such as yours.

MRS. KEMPLER: Why Charles, that is so sweet of you to say.

KEMPLER: Therefore, I beg you to feign a little modesty for the next few months. Perhaps you'll get addicted to it. Something glorious might come of it. What do you think?

MRS. KEMPLER: I think you are very generous.

KEMPLER: *(Pause)* Do you love me, Abril?

MRS. KEMPLER: *(Touchingly direct)* Yes.

KEMPLER: Should I believe you?

MRS. KEMPLER: Yes.

KEMPLER: Is the future bright?

MRS. KEMPLER: The future is always bright.

KEMPLER: Things in the past are forgiven?

MRS. KEMPLER: Best they are.

KEMPLER: I was never shocked.

MRS. KEMPLER: I could swear that you were.

KEMPLER: No. I was never shocked. *(Takes out wallet, drops American Express card on check plate)*

END OF ACT TWO

ACT THREE

(A week later. The COLONEL*'s office in Morocco.* KEMPLER *is at the door, waiting for the* COLONEL*'s attention.)*

KEMPLER: *(Abruptly, wired)* Excuse me, I thought you were free for the evening.

COLONEL: Yes, I thought so as well. Come in, Mr. Kempler. I really didn't expect you to drop by. When you phoned, I was quite surprised.

KEMPLER: I thought it best to phone.

COLONEL: I'm honored that you called. You've been in my thoughts for several days. Come in, come in.

*(*KEMPLER *approaches the* COLONEL.*)*

COLONEL: Tell me, what are you doing here?

KEMPLER: Details.

COLONEL: I thought you left the country?

KEMPLER: Yes, for a short while. We were in Spain.

COLONEL: *(Patronizing)* And how was Spain?

KEMPLER: Quite beguiling actually. May I sit?

*(*COLONEL *gestures.)*

KEMPLER: I see you've painted the office.

COLONEL: Can you tell?

KEMPLER: A fine improvement.

COLONEL: Thank you. My wife chose the color. *(Pause)* Are you here strictly on business?

KEMPLER: The park has opened.

COLONEL: I was waiting for your invitation.

KEMPLER: You didn't miss a thing.

COLONEL: And now what, Mr. Kempler?

KEMPLER: Plans on the continent. Too early to tell. *(Long pause. Awkward.)* My office forwarded your letter.

COLONEL: What letter?

KEMPLER: I should say, your little note.

COLONEL: I sent no note.

KEMPLER: Is that right, Colonel? It was prison stationery.

COLONEL: Mr. Kempler, I have no cause to do such a thing.

KEMPLER: I'm sure you had your reasons.

COLONEL: Reasons?

KEMPLER: Why belabor an unfortunate situation?

COLONEL: You must be dreaming.

KEMPLER: Not at all. My wife must also be dreaming.

COLONEL: I've had a very long day, Mr. Kempler.

KEMPLER: My wife had me see a psychiatrist in Malaga.

COLONEL: Bravo!

KEMPLER: He was quite expensive. Three hundred dirhams a session. I didn't even get full hours.

COLONEL: Why are you telling me this?

KEMPLER: May I smoke?

COLONEL: By all means.

KEMPLER: Colonel, stop these little games.

COLONEL: Mr. Kempler, I've no idea what the hell you're talking about. What games?

KEMPLER: Perhaps I've no tolerance for these things.

COLONEL: I'm a very busy man, from early in the morning. I try to make it easy for myself, and for others. If your building project is finished, why be here at all? Why imagine things that are not so?

Why make faces at me, Mr. Kempler? Why not just have a drink with me? *(Pause)* You look terrible. Are you well?

KEMPLER: Yes, of course.

COLONEL: Is your wife with you?

KEMPLER: Yes, she is.

COLONEL: How is she?

KEMPLER: Fine. Lovely as ever.

COLONEL: I didn't expect you to return to Fez. I thought you had made that clear to me.

KEMPLER: Perhaps I came back on principle.

COLONEL: Excuse me. *(Takes out liquor)* A drink?

KEMPLER: Please.

COLONEL: What can I do for you then?

KEMPLER: Tell me who my wife is?

COLONEL: Your wife is your wife.

KEMPLER: Why not amplify that for me?

COLONEL: Don't be ridiculous, Mr. Kempler. You know your wife much better than I.

KEMPLER: In your note you had no trouble expressing yourself.

COLONEL: Was this note signed by me?

KEMPLER: I'm certain it was yours, Colonel.

COLONEL: And if it was mine, why would you be upset?

KEMPLER: Do I look upset?

COLONEL: What did this note say?

KEMPLER: *(Temper rising)* I worked very hard in Fez. Everyone knows that. I made time for her. We had more than enough time for each other. I know how to be generous.

COLONEL: Are you in trouble?

KEMPLER: Can I have another drink?

COLONEL: Take the bottle.

KEMPLER: *(Pouring from the bottle)* I trust your judgment. Did you know that?

COLONEL: My judgment, Mr. Kempler?

KEMPLER: Tell me, just friend to friend, how would you continue with Abril?

COLONEL: I?

KEMPLER: Would you let her stay the way she was?

COLONEL: Your wife is a gypsy. I don't understand gypsies.

KEMPLER: But you speak her language.

COLONEL: I'm sure she speaks many languages.

KEMPLER: You know her for what she is. A woman like Abril can live without shame. I cannot.

COLONEL: Did you catch her again?

KEMPLER: Yes. Now I can tell by which earrings she has on. Isn't that something? The drop pearls are her little neon lights.

COLONEL: Are you being facetious?

KEMPLER: My wife is an anomaly. Hardly an asset. What would you do in this instance?

COLONEL: What instance?

KEMPLER: You found her with a...

COLONEL: *(Interrupting)* I cannot say.

KEMPLER: Shall I read your mind, Colonel?

COLONEL: Please.

KEMPLER: You would take down your saber. You would torture her, as you did in your jail.

COLONEL: Torture is arcane. You have a strange imagination, Mr. Kempler.

KEMPLER: You would humiliate her beyond need or satisfaction. You would bond her, and brand her like cattle, keep her on a straw mattress without clothes. You would beat her and taunt her with your black riding crop. I know what you really can do, Colonel. Arabs dominate these bitches very well.

COLONEL: You watch too many movies, Mr. Kempler.

KEMPLER: But it's true. These are your priorities. Two Arab brothers would sooner kill a woman, than let her come between them. That is your culture since creation.

COLONEL: Why overpraise my people? We're all thieves and beggars, addicts and murderers. *(Amused)* And you are Dagwood Bumstead. Isn't that so?

KEMPLER: Yes, I am.

COLONEL: It's a comic strip. You sleep on the couch, and the dog barks, and your wife Blondie has purchased a new dress with your seventeen credit cards. *(Pause)* Would you care for another drink? *(Pours two glasses)* Yet your wife Blondie loves you very much. You must know that.

KEMPLER: I don't think so.

COLONEL: You are fooling yourself. Believe me, you are. My religion believes in duty with regard to the wife. She is not a kitchen appliance. She is not disposable as such. But training is expected, and you must do the training. How is that for wisdom?

KEMPLER: Uninspiring.

COLONEL: Yes, forgive me. I am not Mohammed.

KEMPLER: Your advice is late in coming.

COLONEL: And so is the Messiah.

KEMPLER: I cannot afford a shattered marriage. Can you understand that?

COLONEL: You are very gifted, Mr. Kempler. I think you could sustain injury. You have plenty of nerve.

KEMPLER: Do you think so?

COLONEL: If you Jews charade with Gentile names and Gentile faces and Gentile firms, I call that nerve. Nerve to appear unquestionably Jewish. That you worked on your diction and that you admire our mosques and restaurants and women. Nerve to marry one of us, in fact. Yes, you have this incredible trait every waking day. It makes you successful, Mr. Kempler. It's in your every step.

KEMPLER: Thank you for the ridicule.

COLONEL: It is a bouquet to you. *(Pause)* Where is your wife, Mr. Kempler?

KEMPLER: I left her in Spain.

COLONEL: Is she well?

KEMPLER: I don't really care.

COLONEL: You do care.

KEMPLER: No, it's over.

COLONEL: Infidelity can be treated.

KEMPLER: I don't have a claim to her any longer.

COLONEL: Even whores have a state of grace.

KEMPLER: She's another species altogether.

COLONEL: Have children. That is my recommendation. Make babies. A half a dozen to start. *(Pause. Studied look.)* It is heartfelt, Mr. Kempler.

KEMPLER: We can't have children.

COLONEL: *(Sympathetic)* I'm sorry. *(Distracted, perhaps with papers on the desk)* How many men do you think have been with her?

KEMPLER: There were a good many.

COLONEL: Fifty? A hundred?

KEMPLER: Have you a bet with someone?

COLONEL: I'm only trying to get a grasp.

KEMPLER: She's not for hire. She never was.

COLONEL: I didn't insinuate anything.

KEMPLER: I'm not old-fashioned, Colonel.

COLONEL: You're simply a husband.

KEMPLER: Yes, I'm simply a husband. *(Long pause)* I threatened to kill her the night before leaving Malaga.

COLONEL: Did you?

KEMPLER: Our sex life stopped dead.

COLONEL: Was there a sex life at all, Mr. Kempler?

KEMPLER: Yes.

COLONEL: No, no, you can tell me the truth...

KEMPLER: I am.

COLONEL: Are you faithful?

KEMPLER: She cheats. I do not cheat.

COLONEL: We all cheat. *(Pause)* Your wife is from Gibraltar. Once a crazy place. I wish I could be more helpful, Mr. Kempler.

KEMPLER: Actually, you've been very helpful.

COLONEL: Have I?

KEMPLER: I thought you knew that.

COLONEL: I know very little.

KEMPLER: You know me like a glove. I admire you, Colonel. I admire your sense of resolve, and your polite manner. You have a circumspect mind too, and that has not gone by unnoticed. *(Pause)* I would like the photographs back, Colonel.

COLONEL: Yes, as you wish. *(Some physical contact with* KEMPLER*)* But first, why don't we go into the city tonight? You did invite me out. I know a very fine restaurant, Mr. Kempler, with a Sephardic menu. We'll pretend we're two bachelors.

KEMPLER: Why pretend?

COLONEL: You are in a humor. *(Rising)* I'll get my coat. Has your wife been to see the project?

KEMPLER: She was reluctant to go. Sometimes she is superstitious.

COLONEL: Really?

KEMPLER: Women are superstitious, Colonel. You know that. I hope to carry on another project or two on the continent. Tangier. You know how good steady work can be.

COLONEL: I do.

KEMPLER: There's a building recession in my country. Architects must travel. I've come to accept this. Jewish professionals with Berlitz dictionaries and loose cash in their suit pockets. Still, I believe in my profession. Architecture is a benign discipline. Art and engineering. Soul and body. Private and public. Do you see the connection?

COLONEL: No, Mr. Kempler.

KEMPLER: The events over the last few weeks have shaken me. My training hasn't prepared me for you. I thought work was everything. What makes an architect happy? Posterity? Pomposity? We crown ourselves with each difficult creation. Your degree of understanding has moved me. You offer something remedial to my marriage. Your jealousy tipped me off to things, Colonel.

COLONEL: My jealousy?

KEMPLER: If I could lie as skillfully as you, I would be much stronger. I could reverse the damage I've incurred here. I could preserve the shine to my good name. *(Pause)* In the Medina, all the faces are shrouded in anonymity and mystery. I want my face to be branded in your presence. Burned onto your retina.

COLONEL: Clearly, I've offended you, my friend. I thought all was—as you call—judicious and fair. Is there something in this office for you?

KEMPLER: In this office...no.

COLONEL: Then my hands are tied.

KEMPLER: Talk to me.

COLONEL: Dear God, I am talking to you. If I rip your tongue out, Mr. Kempler, you would still get in the last word. Isn't that so?

KEMPLER: What would you say if I told you...

COLONEL: Tell me what?

KEMPLER: If I told you that Mrs. Kempler has disappeared?

COLONEL: Has she? Where has she gone?

KEMPLER: Don't you know? Haven't you been communicating with her?

COLONEL: Mr. Kempler, shall I call the police?

KEMPLER: You are the police.

COLONEL: If the woman has disappeared...

KEMPLER: Don't be clever.

COLONEL: Is she in this city?

KEMPLER: I don't know. We came back together.

COLONEL: That wasn't wise to bring her back, Mr. Kempler.

KEMPLER: I had no choice. She couldn't bear the separation. What was I to do? Lock her in room until Fez was completed? She had something to prove to me. She needed to erase the traces of the scandal. I bought her jewelry. She gave it away to the valet. When the testing stopped, the teasing began. She told the chambermaid in Malaga that I was incontinent. That she had to throw away the sheets. This is her sense of humor. A luxury hotel, no less.

COLONEL: Are you incontinent?

KEMPLER: *(Ironic)* I have never wet a bed in my life.

COLONEL: Why did you marry this woman?

KEMPLER: I don't know. One would think it was from love. I was glad to break from my family, as she broke from hers. She vanquished things mediocre inside me.

COLONEL: She is an instrument of your daily embarrassment. Is this American, Mr. Kempler? Mixing success with the best cow manure? You have magnificent dreams of erecting buildings and parks and monuments, dignity very few men achieve. But in all the time I have known you, I cannot see your dignity.

KEMPLER: Look harder, Colonel. It is there.

COLONEL: You're a stubborn man. As stubborn as she.

KEMPLER: No one spotted her as you had. No one at her office suspected.

COLONEL: They are all whores at the bank.

KEMPLER: I always thought of her as my princess.

COLONEL: Yes, my friend, you married an enchanting storybook princess. Such youth at your age is quite damaging. You will go home, find your delinquent wife, and begin again. Forget your lunch pail. Philosophy can only make a man alchoholic.

KEMPLER: If God were only so kind.

COLONEL: God barters.

KEMPLER: God is barbaric.

COLONEL: Only in the movies.

KEMPLER: Do you go to the movies, Colonel?

COLONEL: Yes, on occasion.

KEMPLER: I only like sad movies.

COLONEL: I like the cowboy movies. We all like the cowboy movies, Mr. Kempler. You ought to try acting like a cowboy. You can make campfire at night, and kiss your horse sweet dreams. You put me in a strange mood tonight. One more drink for the road?

KEMPLER: Thank you.

COLONEL: *(Pouring drinks)* I like you without your necktie.

KEMPLER: Do you?

COLONEL: But you sit like you have a rifle up your trousers.

KEMPLER: It's the overtime at the drafting table.

COLONEL: Drink up, it might be hard to buy drinks outside.

KEMPLER: To yesterday's happiness. *(They drink in unison.)* Are you superstitious, Colonel?

COLONEL: No. Are you?

KEMPLER: I fear shadows which dance on the old city walls. Sometimes I notice clear patterns. It's her portrait. Unmistakeable. More and more it occurred to me that Abril is possessed.

COLONEL: Possessed?

KEMPLER: That the Devil has entered her.

COLONEL: You don't believe that.

KEMPLER: No, of course not.

COLONEL: It is a stupid belief.

KEMPLER: Many people believe otherwise.

COLONEL: Surely not you.

KEMPLER: Only the Devil can alter someone.

COLONEL: Please, no ghost stories this evening. Your wife is not possessed. It is out of the question. She is too intelligent to be possessed. *(Pause)* Where is your wife, Mr. Kempler?

KEMPLER: I killed her.

COLONEL: Where is your wife?

KEMPLER: You should know.

COLONEL: Where is she, Mr. Kempler?

KEMPLER: Hell, for all I care. You needn't act bewildered.

COLONEL: Why do you persist with this joke?

KEMPLER: Take down my confession, Colonel. I'll make it easy for you. Friend to friend.

COLONEL: Don't make a fool of me.

KEMPLER: Her body is still warm in the hotel room.

COLONEL: Here in Fez?

KEMPLER: Yes.

COLONEL: Very amusing, Mr. Kempler. *(Silence)* You never told me how you met your wife.

KEMPLER: We met a dozen years ago at a building project. She represented the banking committee. She was different then. Very chaste. Very supportive. Very soft and fragile. I fell for her at once. When I started courting her I did miraculous things. Expenses meant nothing to me. We acted like schoolchildren on holiday. She was so pristine in daylight. So open to my clumsiness. Patient with my faults. What little faults I had. Things were simpler then.

COLONEL: As for us all.

KEMPLER: Dear God. Sex alone could not destroy my wife.

COLONEL: I don't know what does destroy a woman. Perhaps it is rich living. Perhaps she has taken the worst your world has provided for her. Perhaps she is possessed by your Devil. She cannot be taught to be another way. Not her. That is plain. Devil or no Devil. *(Long pause)* How did you murder Mrs. Kempler?

KEMPLER: I picked up a clothes iron.

COLONEL: Was death instantaneous?

KEMPLER: I think so.

COLONEL: *(A difficult pause)* Any struggle?

KEMPLER: None.

COLONEL: Look at me, Mr. Kempler. *(Pause)* Did you actually have the courage to do it?

KEMPLER: Does it matter? Did she mean anything to you?

COLONEL: As long as you're confessing...

KEMPLER: It was as though I were sleepwalking. I paced the hotel room afterwards looking for loose coins that I had thrown at her. I unwrapped all of the hotel soap, showered vigorously, lunched on the balcony alone, and then dressed to go out.

COLONEL: Why do you patronize me? You don't have the courage to kill a housefly, Mr. Kempler. I doubt that you would even raise a hand to your wife.

KEMPLER: I would agree with you, but the truth is...

COLONEL: But the truth is that you are impotent to act.

KEMPLER: Believe what you want.

COLONEL: That is all I can do.

KEMPLER: I am not a coward. I would gladly do it again.

COLONEL: Mr. Kempler, your concerns are dear to me. I wish I had medicine for you. This isn't pity. You should have married a Jew as you were no doubt instructed since birth. You would be happier today. Yes, I'm certain of it. I think your blindness is in very poor taste. I don't think you can help yourself either. Do not try to impress me. I pray for you and your wife. If you have done something wrong, do not make me an accomplice.

KEMPLER: I don't need an accomplice.

COLONEL: But you are pointing at me.

KEMPLER: I don't need an accomplice, Colonel. I did everything alone. I stained the bedsheets with her blood and poured her liquid mascara over the head wounds. It was the best that I could do. I couldn't hear her cry. I couldn't explain to her the meaning of her punishment. I couldn't express myself to my wife with more urgency than with a shot to the head. It really was the best that I could do. She sat in the hotel lobby all evening, and there were complaints from the management. I had to carry her upstairs. Yes, she was drunk. Some men were following her. Conversation was impossible. How pathetic we were. I dropped her over the hotel bed. She kicked off her shoes. *(Pause)* And then I killed her.

COLONEL: Must you spoil my evening?

KEMPLER: No, I had no intention of spoiling your evening.

COLONEL: I did not hear any of this.

KEMPLER: There is nothing you did not hear. And there is nothing that you did not see. You can't hurt me anymore. *(MRS. KEMPLER enters, first seen by the COLONEL and then KEMPLER.)*

MRS. KEMPLER: Charles... *(KEMPLER reacts.)* I want you home. Please come home with me. *(Pause)* Darling...

KEMPLER: Why did you come here?

MRS. KEMPLER: I came for you.

KEMPLER: Go. I'll meet you outside.

MRS. KEMPLER: Only if you come with me.

KEMPLER: I can't believe your timing.

COLONEL: Go home, Mr. Kempler. It's time I closed the office. *(Pause. Awkward.)* How nice to see you, Mrs. Kempler. Your husband's very entertaining.

MRS. KEMPLER: Charles?

COLONEL: He has certain obsessions, Mrs. Kempler. Obsessions for storytelling.

MRS. KEMPLER: It's an old Semitic tradition...storytelling. How good we all are at it. *(Pause)* Shall I tell a story? In a land bound in tradition, a woman is thrown behind bars. To each man stands a ridiculous claim. It is a tangled story. Is she whore or blessed wife? She loves her husband. Reaches out for him again. A second marriage which restores the first. Grant her wish? Love. Renewal. An everlasting vow. If he reconsiders, Scheherazade is spared another night. Until tomorrow. Until death's blade. Until tomorrow. *(Pause)* Are you content?

KEMPLER: *(Dignified restraint)* Yes.

MRS. KEMPLER: *(Pause)* Any further business?

KEMPLER: *(Approaching her)* No further business.

MRS. KEMPLER: *(Turning to* COLONEL*)* Did you say anything wrong to my husband? (COLONEL *is silent, expressionless.)* Wash kedebti-L-rajali? ("Did you say anything wrong to my husband?")

COLONEL: La Abadan ("No. Never.")

MRS. KEMPLER: Wakha. Kul shi mezyen. ("Fine. Everything is all right.")

COLONEL: Ma Kaynsh sabab. Barakallafikum. ("There would be no reason. God's blessing on you.") God's blessing on you.

MRS. KEMPLER: *(Walking slowly to* KEMPLER *to exit)* Charles... *(They are now arm in arm.)*

COLONEL: *(With off-handed charm)* Do visit us again.

MRS. KEMPLER: As far as I'm concerned, we never met.

COLONEL: As you wish.

MRS. KEMPLER: *(Lingering moment)* Maa-sa-lama. ("Goodbye.")

COLONEL: *(Stirring to best posture)* Maa-sa-lama, Mrs. Kempler. *(After a beat, retrieving envelope of photographs for* KEMPLER, *extending hand)* Mr. Kempler... (KEMPLER *makes no effort to receive photos.* COLONEL's *hand drops slowly as lights fade to blackout.)*

END OF PLAY

HOSPITALITY

ORIGINAL PRODUCTIONS

Philadelphia Theater Company, first performance 10 April 1988:

HAPPY . . . . Larry Pine
FULLER . . . . Herb Downer
CORTEZ . . . . Patricia Mauceri
AGUNEIR . . . . Ronald Hunter
MONTEITH . . . . Robert Trumbull

Director . . . . William Foeller

London: N.A./U.K. at the Viceroy Pub, first performance 24 January 1989:

HAPPY . . . . Stephen Hoye
FULLER . . . . Neville Aurelius
CORTEZ . . . . Lesley Joseph
AGUNEIR . . . . Norman Chancer
MONTEITH . . . . Ed Bishop

Director . . . . Lisa Forrell

CHARACTERS

HAPPY—*male, 40s, white, Immigration Agent*
FULLER—*male, 40s, black, Immigration Agent*
CORTEZ—*female, 30s, Spanish journalist from Colombia*
AGUNEIR—*male, 50s, Israeli politician*
MONTEITH—*male, 50s, white, Immigration Supervisor from Washington*

SETTING

A detention center in New York City. The rooms are ascetic and bare. There is a lounge for the agents and a conference room.

The time is 1986.

SCENE ONE

(Day One: CORTEZ'*s room)*

HAPPY: Let's not fool ourselves...a vegetarian lives longer, has finer bowel movements, and maintains a superior memory. You keep friends, have better breath, and lend an undeniable kindness to the animal kingdom. I read this in a clinic in Geneva when I de-toxed. Raw or cooked, you're better off this way. When I glanced at your files, I was glad to recognize an ally in the kitchen. Miss Cortez, I am your ally. And your secret admirer. *(Pause)* You're a very attractive woman, if I may say. Are you hungry?

CORTEZ: No.

HAPPY: Thirsty? *(Pause)* I trust you're comfortable? Room service, cable TV, a wet bar, Kleenexes, just like a hotel... efficiently run. In a day or two, you may wish to dine downstairs in the commons. That's where we all eat. It's more social that way. Better for one's psychology. *(Pause)* They've assigned me to you. Frankly, it's quite an honor. You're a renowned poet and author. A playwright and actor. An inspired leader to our people. I hope I won't be a nuisance, Miss Cortez. I'm here to sort out the mess. *(Pause)* I was supposed to read your works yesterday, but my wife had chores for me. Still, my assistants have perused them, in Spanish and English....Their notes are disturbing. You don't rhyme, Miss Cortez. You use vulgar images for comic affect. And your literature insults men. American men. Well, I won't fault you for that. I really can't. Poetic license.

CORTEZ: I'm not a poet. I am a journalist.

HAPPY: What?

CORTEZ: Idiot. You mistake me for someone else.

HAPPY: Your name is Cortez? Sophia Margarite Cortez?

CORTEZ: Yes.

HAPPY: But you're not the Peruvian poet and actor?

CORTEZ: I am a Colombian journalist. Read your files.

HAPPY: How can this be? It says in my report...

CORTEZ: I'm here by invitation of Harvard University. My papers are in order. You have my passport and visa. I cannot protest enough about this infringement.

HAPPY: We've a new girl on staff, Miss Cortez, and perhaps some papers were shuffled. Perhaps we've confused you with Angelica Cordoba?

CORTEZ: I think you have.

HAPPY: Yes, yes. Cordoba writes plays. You write hoary leftist essays. It says so right here. Well, well, I must look like a horse's ass. Shall we start over again? *(Broad smile)* My name is Happy. Agent Logan. We like first names at Immigration. Relax, Miss Cortez. A vegetarian lives longer, has finer bowel movements, and maintains a superior memory. Raw or cooked, you're better off this way. You are a vegetarian?

CORTEZ: Idiot.

HAPPY: Wrong again. You eat meat, don't you, Miss Cortez? We'll feed you meat. *(Pause)* Various groups have petitioned on your behalf. You're a celebrity. I'm in awe of celebrities. Does that make you feel happy? *(Pause)* You've very alluring eyes, Miss Cortez. Like harden diamonds in moonlight. They are the window into your soul. A privilege to see. Dear God, am I blushing? *(Pause)* I was told you know your rights, and that the McCarran-Walter Act was explained. Good. We can forgo the long preamble. My government created McCarran-Walter to skim garbage off the surface of our shores. Senator McCarthy would be pleased to see the law thriving. It is a good law. According to my files, you don't belong here. You did wrong, Miss Cortez. You should have remained on the plane.

CORTEZ: My papers are in order.

HAPPY: The visa was issued in error. We wrote you, Miss Cortez. As an officer of Immigration and Naturalization, I wish to apologize for this incontrovertible error.

CORTEZ: Apologize?

HAPPY: The visa was rescinded. Tough luck.

CORTEZ: What are you afraid of? What has happened to America?

HAPPY: America has gotten stronger. More confident. *(Pause)* Are you a reporter for *El Tiempo* in Bogota? *(Pause)* It would help your case enormously, if you answer the questions. Are you a...

CORTEZ: Yes.

HAPPY: How many years?

CORTEZ: Eleven.

HAPPY: You don't look that old.

CORTEZ: I'm thirty-seven.

HAPPY: Any children?

CORTEZ: No.

HAPPY: Your time clock is ticking, Miss Cortez.

CORTEZ: Don't lecture me, Mr. Logan.

HAPPY: Are you a friend of democracy?

CORTEZ: I would hope so.

HAPPY: Do you know the meaning of democracy?

CORTEZ: More thoroughly than you.

HAPPY: Miss Cortez, are you an astrologist? Do you read Jeane Dixon? *(Pause)* Miss Cortez, are you engaged in subversive activities in your native land? *(Pause)* Miss Cortez, do you like detention?

CORTEZ: Freedom is better than prison.

HAPPY: Exactly. Work with me, Miss Cortez. As a vegetarian I believe in tempered living. The golden mean. Christian sobriety. Are you a member of a Colombian group known as M-19?

CORTEZ: No.

HAPPY: Are you a Cuban agent?

CORTEZ: I am Jesus' sister.

HAPPY: I thought so. It says in my report that you served as a liaison between M-19 and the Cuban secret police.

CORTEZ: I resent your accusations, Mr. Logan.

HAPPY: The M-19 assaulted the Palace of Justice. Several deaths and many injuries. Play ball with us, Miss Cortez. In a few days you're expected at Harvard.

CORTEZ: I want my ambassador.

HAPPY: Tell me you plan to cooperate, Miss Cortez.

CORTEZ: You shall not muzzle me.

HAPPY: Cooperate. Say it. Please.

CORTEZ: *(Pause)* I want to cooperate.

HAPPY: I believe you, Miss Cortez. My report says you're a renowned columnist. Shrewd. Skillful. Tell me the truth. I know your wrongdoing. Your sins. My instructions are to crack you. I'm very good at this. I've many questions to ask you. Today. Tomorrow. The next day. Until the day I pour wine. I've other detainees waiting. You are number one. Prize catch in the net. Talk to me, Miss Cortez...

CORTEZ: What do you care to know?

HAPPY: Are you a virgin?

CORTEZ: Are you an imbecile?

HAPPY: Flatter my intelligence, Miss Cortez. I had a year of college. Are you a member of M-19?

CORTEZ: I want my lawyer.

HAPPY: We're holding your lawyer in the other cell. I hate his cologne. You'll see him. I'd like to know about your personal life. Your personal contacts.

CORTEZ: I'm certain you have them in your reports.

HAPPY: I want names. Don't bother listing the academics. Men with guns. Names we fear. *(Starts tape recorder)* Go ahead, Miss Cortez.

CORTEZ: Go to hell.

HAPPY: It's my job, lovey.

CORTEZ: Are you so afraid of me, Mr. Logan.

HAPPY: Do I seem afraid?

CORTEZ: Like a weasel, yes.

HAPPY: I'm not an animal, Miss Cortez.

CORTEZ: Scatch your private parts at home.

HAPPY: Give me ten names. That's all. And that will make me happy.

CORTEZ: You'll get no names.

HAPPY: Miss Cortez, now is the time to speak your mind.

CORTEZ: I don't like your administration's policies in Latin America. Your tacit support of Chile. The way your banks treat us. The deals made with El Salvador. The trade war with Cuba. Your games with Ortega and the Contras.

HAPPY: Have you killed people, Miss Cortez? Have you taught others to kill? Have you spent any time in Cuba? Did you have an affair with Gabriel Marquez at the Hilton in Buenos Aires? What is your sordid relationship with former President Belesario Bentancur? May we see an advance text of your Harvard address?

CORTEZ: Fuck off, Mr. Logan.

HAPPY: I provoked a reaction. Forgive me. The tape was on. *(Turns off recorder)* May we please see an advance text, Miss Cortez?

CORTEZ: You've confiscated all my papers.

HAPPY: We could not find the Harvard address.

CORTEZ: For a free nation, your actions...

HAPPY: Are you a communist, Miss Cortez?

CORTEZ: No, Mr. Logan.

HAPPY: A Marxist? A spider woman from Cuba? Is it true that you've served on the ruling committee of M-19?

CORTEZ: No.

HAPPY: Since we're getting nowhere, why not just give me some names, and we can stop this charade.

CORTEZ: For you?

HAPPY: Yes. For me. Because I sense that you secretly like me.

CORTEZ: Like you?

HAPPY: You know what I mean. *(Pause)* Some names. *(Pause)* Miss Cortez?

CORTEZ: All right. (HAPPY *turns on tape.*) Rockefeller...Forbes...
Trump...Hunt...Getty...

HAPPY: *(Turns off tape)* Splendid. *(Pause)* Do you want a spanking?
(Pause)

CORTEZ: I don't think I can satisfy you with this interrogation.

HAPPY: I should have been assigned to Cordoba. All I want is
cooperation. *(Pause)* I was a postal employee for six years before
getting transferred. My brother-in-law moved me into Immigration.
Said the money was worth it. He didn't mention the aggravation.
Don't add to my aggravation. Miss Cortez, keep me happy. I know
you can.

CORTEZ: I'm here to aggravate you.

HAPPY: Why did you choose to become a journalist?

CORTEZ: My father was a journalist.

HAPPY: Do you know Leonard Bernstein?

CORTEZ: No.

HAPPY: Ted Kennedy? Jane Fonda? Our agents discovered that you
also had an appointment to visit East Hampton, Long Island. Can
you corroborate that for me? It's off season in the Hamptons, Miss
Cortez. What business do you have out there?

CORTEZ: A friend of my husband's has a country house.

HAPPY: A rich friend, no doubt?

CORTEZ: Richer than myself, yes.

HAPPY: You want publicity, to become a cause celibrè?

CORTEZ: No, Mr. Logan.

HAPPY: You want to beat me, outsmart me. I can read your thoughts,
Miss Cortez. I'm a formidable individual. I have your pulse. I feel the
inexorable heat radiating from inside you. The Spanish paranoia in
your voice. Give me credit for understanding you. For hunting you
inside a small room. *(Silence; smiling warmly)* Again, I only want
names from you. What a simple deal it would be, if you only agreed
to play the game. The game is simple, Miss Cortez. Come play the
game.

SCENE TWO

(Day One: Adjacent room — AGUNEIR's cell)

AGUNEIR: Give me a cigarette.

FULLER: Here.

AGUNEIR: Match.

FULLER: On the table.

AGUNEIR: How long will this go on?

FULLER: I don't know.

AGUNEIR: You know. Cut the nonsense.

FULLER: JDL?

AGUNEIR: I'm not responsible for them.

FULLER: They were once your group.

AGUNEIR: Not now.

FULLER: There was a bombing last night. Cooperate, Aguneir.

AGUNEIR: I am an American.

FULLER: You hold two passports.

AGUNEIR: I was born in New York.

FULLER: You're an Israeli officer in the Knesset.

AGUNEIR: Until there's a change in the law, I am an American.

FULLER: Tell me, my friend, why you became violent at the airport? You punched out one of our officers. You were warned not to come.

AGUNEIR: Where is my insulin?

FULLER: Coming shortly.

AGUNEIR: I take it now, Fuller.

FULLER: Within the hour. What makes you an American? Your self-righteousness?

AGUNEIR: The Bible, you little asshole.

FULLER: Do you know the Bible so well?

AGUNEIR: I was an ordained rabbi.

FULLER: Hard to believe.

AGUNEIR: Give me another cigarette.

FULLER: Take the pack.

AGUNEIR: You look at me with mockery.

FULLER: It's unintentional.

AGUNEIR: I'm not a madman.

FULLER: Prove it.

AGUNEIR: I'll walk on water.

FULLER: Tell me about the bombings.

AGUNEIR: There are bombings in Paris. Am I responsible?

FULLER: The Atlantic Avenue restaurant.

AGUNEIR: A diner's flatulence, I'm sure. I was in Israel during this period.

FULLER: What about the Defense League?

AGUNEIR: No contact with them in five years.

FULLER: You're full of shit.

AGUNEIR: All my energy is in Israel. You know that. Why are you keeping me here? Where is my insulin? When do I see my attorney Loveberg? I have friends in this city. Powerful friends. Soon I'll get on the phone.

FULLER: You call yourself the King of Israel.

AGUNEIR: No. Begin did.

FULLER: You're a lowlife.

AGUNEIR: I'm a glorious Sephardic saint. Get on your filthy knees. Where is your superior? Enough with this merry-go-round. I'm an important statesman. Get out of my way. Understand? Nod your head if you do. Give me your superior.

FULLER: You must deal with me. (Pause) Tell me about the munitions depot. Who was in charge?

AGUNEIR: An angel on earth. A pornographer from Beirut. Enough questions. I have no patience for this. Give me dinner. And then a clean taxi. I must go. And my insulin. I will call the Congressman from Long Island. I will punish you, God help you if you dally. I'm not a man of peace, I am a dark angel.

FULLER: What makes you a dark angel?

AGUNEIR: The world's a very sick place. *(Pause)* Who else have you locked here? *(Pause)* You should lock up Farrahkan. He hides a missile under his bow tie. Hitler's stepchild. Take racism where you find it.

FULLER: There's a rash of bombings with your visit.

AGUNEIR: There are bombings because people lack entertainment. They have no spiritual direction. Money can extend so far. Stick out your tongue, Fuller. Let's see how far you extend. (AGUNEIR *sticks out his tongue with obscene noise.*) I'm a religious leader lest you forget. And a hardcore politician. I can make the rudest secular noises you ever heard. I am the new noise in Israel. Why? Because I say what people hide in their hearts. Because I herald from Brooklyn's Crown Heights. Keep me locked up, you help my publicity. Tell me what will you accomplish? I have a moral agenda. You have an obscene shopping list.

FULLER: Give me a hint about the cash funds from Jersey. The loan guarantees are in your name.

AGUNEIR: My name is artificial. Any guarantees are artificial. I am self-invented. Pygmalion by Pygmalion. My family name was Shulman. People use my name for fund raising. My name attracts money. As it should. I know you want to lay a trap for me. Go ahead. You're dealing with a stubborn old man. I'll wait you out. I am spirit, you see. You are clay. *(Pause)* I want to see a newspaper, Fuller. Quick. Here's some change, go and buy a paper. What is the press saying about this? Do they know? Are they on your side, or mine?

FULLER: No newspapers.

AGUNEIR: Thief!

FULLER: Am I?

AGUNEIR: Where is my wristwatch?

FULLER: Did you have a wristwatch?

AGUNEIR: Yes. On the table.

FULLER: I don't have it.

AGUNEIR: It was given to me by my grandfather. Empty your Goddamn pockets.

FULLER: Enough.

AGUNEIR: There's a putrid smell in this room.

FULLER: I think it's time to straighten you out. You're not in Israel. While you're here, you must give answers. I'm running out of patience. And that's a bad thing. You can only start trouble here. I'm not a negotiator. I don't bargain. There have been a dozen bombings in the last month. JDL related. And now you're here. The timing stinks. Bombs going off like roman candles in the night. Something's scaring this city, and we're going to eradicate it. *(Pause)* I don't like you Aguneir. I don't like your blatant supremacy airs. You look very ugly to me. It's the pathology of your rabid face which I hate.

AGUNEIR: You've no reason to hate me.

FULLER: You're a racist and demigogue.

AGUNEIR: I'm a member of clergy. I herd my flock.

FULLER: Such garbage with no love in your heart.

AGUNEIR: Not true. I love all people. Rich and poor. White and Black. I love you.

FULLER: Do you?

AGUNEIR: Ethiopians are my brethren. You may be a Jew, Fuller. Come, I'll circumcise you.

FULLER: *(Leaving bag on table; rising)* You're an actor from Hell. When I come back, I want some answers about these punks in your old neighborhood. It can be much easier to comply. Talk quickly, and with respect. *(Exiting)* Your insulin is in the bag.

SCENE THREE

(Second day: CORTEZ's *room)*

HAPPY: You look like my wife's sister, Miss Cortez. A little arrogant and heavy on the eye shadow. It's the way you drum your fingers on the table. And your garish nail polish. My wife's sister has a piercing cold stare. Right to my heart. She eats men and spits them out like cherry pits. Not my idea of a dream girl.

CORTEZ: What is your idea of a dream girl, Mr. Logan?

HAPPY: I like my slippers brought to the foot of the bed.

CORTEZ: Get a German shepherd.

HAPPY: My dream girl would be someone who brings me inner peace. Like the girls from the Orient. Someone to draw the warm bath. And keep evil spirits from the front door. An angel who doesn't spend a ton of money. But you see, Miss Cortez, I'm already married. Surely you've noticed my wedding ring? *(Pause)* A woman should flatter the opposite sex. As you are, I'm sure, quite capable of doing. Because you are the smarter sex. I've always felt that. You know the weaknesses in men. You know the subtleties of psychology. Isn't that so? How can I compete with you in this arena? *(Pause)* Tell me, Miss Cortez, why would Harvard honor you if you're known in astute circles as Castro's ass-licking whore?

CORTEZ: And you bend over for Reagan.

HAPPY: He's my president.

CORTEZ: He's living a movie. I think that's dangerous.

HAPPY: I think your radicalism is dangerous.

CORTEZ: My radicalism is in print. I don't shoot people.

HAPPY: What do you do in bed?

CORTEZ: What do you do in the bathroom, Mr. Logan?

HAPPY: I read the newspaper. *(Pause)* Did you ever perform fellatio in public on an Army rifle? Smile, Miss Cortez. Behind that mirror, there's a camera on you. Because when you're gone, I'll have something of you still with me. I'm a collector. And you will have joined my collection. *(Pause)* Your profile in black and white. Your fingers tapping the wood. No one in the room but you. You put on a different face alone. A face of insecurity.

CORTEZ: I must be human, Mr. Logan.

HAPPY: Indeed you are. *(Pause)* Miss Cortez, you look drowsy today. Is it that time of month? Would you like Midol? *(Pause)* We're going to make a deal with you. We want you to attend Harvard's convocation. Escorted, first class, cocktails and dinner. All this provided by Immigration.

CORTEZ: What's the deal?

HAPPY: I get to be your handsome escort.

CORTEZ: You?

HAPPY: Because I volunteered. And we're going to dress you in new clothes, because we've ripped your dresses.

CORTEZ: Why are you changing tactics?

HAPPY: Does it seem that way?

CORTEZ: It would be scandalous to your administration if I fail to show.

HAPPY: No, Miss Cortez.

CORTEZ: You inept Boy Scout.

HAPPY: I had a very unhappy childhood. Does it show?

CORTEZ: I want to see a newspaper.

HAPPY: When we go to the airport.

CORTEZ: Let my ambassador escort me.

HAPPY: Your ambassador?

CORTEZ: He's a political conservative. What could be safer?

HAPPY: I think you're a dangerous communist, Miss Cortez. Alarms go off in my head. The world may applaud your writing, but it is a free world which I seek to maintain. I must escort you to protect your freedom of speech. Call it magnamity. A special leniency. Thank me when my job is done.

CORTEZ: You're a blithering idiot.

HAPPY: And what are you, Miss Cortez?

CORTEZ: A Social Democrat.

HAPPY: If I slap your lovely powdered face, a red soldier would feel pain. Who is the real underdog, Miss Cortez? Who is the pretender?

CORTEZ: I'll make certain this incident is made known.

HAPPY: Take out an ad in *The New York Times*.

CORTEZ: Harvard will suffice.

HAPPY: You'll accept the prize from a wheelchair. Word is out that you fell in the shower. Because of painkillers, you cannot speak.

CORTEZ: Even if you gag me, this will explode in your face.

HAPPY: And you're such a fine writer to take on the subject. You're a pert gal, Miss Cortez. I really wish you were on our side. Really, with a little encouragement, I would nuzzle you. Entreat your husband. Have children. Isn't that what nature wants of you? Obedience and fertility. Put down your pen and start breast feeding. Politics is too costly. *(Pause)* I would like to take you on a walking tour of the city. Show you the Staten Island Ferry and the harbor. But you look at me with such disdain. *(Pause)* We're moving you to a new room for the rest of the weekend. You'll have a window with a view of the courtyard. You'll see a delightful French marble.

CORTEZ: I'm not going to Harvard with you, Mr. Logan.

HAPPY: Dinner plans tonight will be a gala affair. Some dignitaries from Washington want to meet you. To convince you to see the good things in the United States. Senator Helms and friends. They want a door to your special world, Miss Cortez. Give them entrance. They want good things for Colombia. See them. It would be a feather in my cap.

CORTEZ: Perhaps there's another arrangement more dignified, Mr. Logan? Dignity is why I write, why I breathe. Can you understand the word?

HAPPY: Dignity...no one can take from you.

CORTEZ: You have no dignity, Mr. Logan. What did you do to Cordoba?

HAPPY: A deal very similar to yours.

CORTEZ: Did she approve?

HAPPY: Go ask her. You may be eating dinner together alfresco.

CORTEZ: With Cordoba?

HAPPY: Yes, under candlelight on an elegant white table cloth, with missing body parts of guerrilla fighters.

CORTEZ: Your jokes are obscene.

HAPPY: Better obscene than dated.

CORTEZ: Better obscene than dead.

HAPPY: Who's dead, Miss Cortez?

CORTEZ: A friend in Bogota. An assassination. Seven bullets to the head. A brother to my brother.

HAPPY: I'm very sorry. Death never comes justly.

CORTEZ: In my hometown, we have a tradition of walking to the ocean for the New Year. Everyone takes this walk. We walk at night, for the certain belief that our sins will wash into the sea. We all believe this. It seems to make us feel better inside. I miss this tradition, Mr. Logan. It is something which I lost when I became a journalist. My loss. *(Pause)* In my hometown we have a saying: To know your deed, know your partner. It always made little sense to me. Always. My mind gets cranky, and bitter. I don't want to become another burnt cynic. I'm very angry inside. Angry at Yankee games with our economy and autonomy. My dearest friends are getting killed.

HAPPY: Get off your soap box.

CORTEZ: Get off my back. I'm no threat to you, Mr. Logan.

HAPPY: You're like Joan of Arc with castanets.

CORTEZ: Send me back to Colombia. I owe you no favor. This investigation is over.

HAPPY: Solitude is yours for the asking. Listen to your heels in the corner of the night, grind your teeth through insomnia. Suffer for your vanity.

CORTEZ: Don't eye me, Mr. Logan.

HAPPY: Your beauty charms me. You've a swan's neck. *(He touches her neck. She slaps him.)* Under different circumstances, I would wine you and dine you. Court you like Sir Walter Raleigh. I am a romantic. Ballroom dancing and moonlight serenades. Tempting the low hem of your skirt, fluffing your pleats, spreading your natural wings. Sing poetry in your Latin ear. Tonight our cook is serving paella on yellow rice.

CORTEZ: Look away, Mr. Logan. I am a married woman. It means something to me. I expect to be in Colombia soon. This turgid affair has gone on too long. Insults bear stupidity. You must act quickly or lose your prey. I've no more patience for your cheapness. Act quickly with me. Or else. Comprende?

SCENE FOUR

(Continuation, Second day: AGUNEIR's *room)*

FULLER: Game Three of the World Series is on tonight. I'm not going to babysit for you, my man. We need to work real quick. *(Pause)* A congressman came today. We told him you had returned to Jerusalem. He believed us. You think we act like dime-store detectives, and suddenly we fulfill your expectations.

AGUNEIR: When I'm through with you, Fuller, you'll be a waiter in the Catskills.

FULLER: I'll kick your ass, pal. It gives me satisfaction to detain a bigot with such small gonads.

AGUNEIR: I am no bigot.

FULLER: But you want to expel the Palestinians.

AGUNEIR: They have cousin states. Israel is for Jews.

FULLER: What sort of Jew are you?

AGUNEIR: I am a rabbi. Yes, a learned man. I could teach you Talmud, or self-defense. Soul and armor. I could beat your brains out. Listen to me, Fuller, I've family waiting. Release me. I'll sing your name to Heaven and I'll grease your palm.

FULLER: I understand you have a girlfriend in the city.

AGUNEIR: And if I do?

FULLER: Tell me what she's like.

AGUNEIR: She's uniquely feminine.

FULLER: Is she political?

AGUNEIR: I just told you, bozo. She's very feminine.

FULLER: I understand she likes rough games.

AGUNEIR: Fuck yourself.

FULLER: Do you like rough games, Rabbi? Is it in the Talmud?

AGUNEIR: Don't play with me, yo yo.

FULLER: We're going to move you to another place, Aguneir.

AGUNEIR: You need to hide me. You're losing.

FULLER: I never lose.

AGUNEIR: The congressman from Long Island will find me. And then you'll be thrown on your black ass.

FULLER: Why did you come to New York?

AGUNEIR: To see my girl and get laid.

FULLER: She thinks you should fly back to Israel. You're begging for trouble. It's not a good year for certain Jews.

AGUNEIR: I'm not a certain Jew.

FULLER: I think your girlfriend makes a whole lot of sense.

AGUNEIR: I don't like advice from colored people.

FULLER: Aguneir, we're going to hold you until hell freezes over. Until your attitude improves. And I will gloat.

AGUNEIR: Do you have the heart to gloat?

FULLER: Watch me.

AGUNEIR: I think you're chicken shit. You remind me of a group of people in Israel. You remind me of the cab drivers in their stained tank tops. You remind me of the discount merchants. You remind me of the lackeys in the civilian army. Your ludicrous bravado. You're a jackass of dubious talents. Little gut. No class. A low-level traffic cop. But you have that affinity for cheap prizes and vulgarity. I am not a cheap prize. Get that through your knappy black head. I am not garbage. In this room, you share space with a very holy man. Genuflect, like a good cocksucker, and get out of my life.

FULLER: *(Firmly, but restrained)* Well, time's up. Get your things, Aguneir. Put them inside that paper bag. Quickly. We're moving your ass now. You'll miss this room. Believe me, you will.

SCENE FIVE

(Day Three: Staff Lounge)

FULLER: Watching the World Series? Big upset.

HAPPY: Got money on the game?

FULLER: Couple of bucks. Why so down?

HAPPY: I'm all right. Wearing new shoes. Like the fashion? Italian look.

FULLER: Italian?

HAPPY: Yeah, Italian. Pinches like shit, but looks great. Thought my wife would like me in them. I'm sick of looking like a slob. You're as good as you look. As good as you feel. I look at your shoes, Fuller, and you know what I see?

FULLER: What?

HAPPY: No ambition.

FULLER: From my shoes?

HAPPY: No shit.

FULLER: I like my shoes.

HAPPY: And you know what? Your vests are out of style. You look like a train conductor, Fuller. Come on. I'll take you shopping. I know a good chink tailor on Essex Street. I hate expensive clothes. If you got the right crease in your trouser...the right fold over the shoe...the right roll of the lapel....I'm talking about sophistication in a worsted blend. And shirts with French cuffs. Clothes you wouldn't dare perspire in. *(Pause)* Hey, Fuller, do you think I shop at Barney's? Do you think I shoplift?

FULLER: Coffee?

HAPPY: Yeah.

FULLER: You look preoccupied.

HAPPY: Me?

FULLER: You.

HAPPY: Preoccupied?

FULLER: Yeah.

HAPPY: It's been three days.

FULLER: Any progress?

HAPPY: Only with the spic.

FULLER: Cordoba?

HAPPY: The other broad, Cortez, La Bruja with the serpent's tongue.

FULLER: How hard you drilling?

HAPPY: Shit, I've been too gentle. I might spike her food. And you?

FULLER: No rough stuff. All routine.

HAPPY: Though I wouldn't kick her out of bed, you know what I mean? Saucy dish. Would love to dive into her muff. You know the fantasy. A little souvenir. *(Produces pink panties to his nose)* From her hamper. A fragrance for Oscar de la Renta.

FULLER: Right.

HAPPY: When are you up for vacation?

FULLER: December, for the holidays.

HAPPY: Lucky you.

FULLER: I received a call from a few congressmen. Another sub-committee survey.

HAPPY: Are they coming?

FULLER: Yes.

HAPPY: Fuck 'em all. Every asshole wants to be a reformer. Just what we need.

FULLER: Show and tell time.

HAPPY: Put on a clean necktie, Fuller. Bark on cue. They want shiny smiles.

FULLER: I won't be able to crack Aguneir in time.

HAPPY: The Jew's a real prick.

FULLER: You bet.

HAPPY: Son of a bitch. We ought to play "Hava Nagilah" on a tape loop. Drive the kike nuts. Or feed him pork.

FULLER: If this goes another day or two, I'm sending him back.

HAPPY: Then your average slips. We're on the big board, Fuller.

FULLER: I know, Happy.

HAPPY: My average's gone up five months straight. Fuller, I'm on a fucking roll. Going to get some big mother perks this Christmas.

FULLER: Don't flaunt it, okay?

HAPPY: I'm enjoying myself. Makes all the difference. We've a noble cause, to protect our Constitution. The subversive element will outspend us, outsmart us, always outrage us. Got to draw the line. God bless our country. As caretakers to her gate, we must keep a vigilant eye and an iron hand. And you must enjoy the challenge...be he terrorist, commie, or Jew.

FULLER: Where does it say we must bust heads?

HAPPY: I don't make the rules, and you're no rookie, babe.

FULLER: When I took this job, Hooper broke me in. Said to play fair. We have authority to weed out the bad apples. No one mentioned cracking to the breaking point. He mentioned civil liberties.

HAPPY: For citizens. For harmless visitors. For us, cracking is everything. Otherwise we're custom officials. You need smarts. Cracking is a surgical skill. A pogrom against the mind of our enemies. Asserts our rights to govern in a hostile world. You know they do this to our people.

FULLER: Yeah.

HAPPY: Daniloff in Moscow. Hausenfaus in Nicaragua. Terbin in Korea. They bomb our embassies, freeze our Swiss bank accounts, make fools of our Marines. Cracking immunes us from political disease.

FULLER: *(Sarcastic)* Run for office, Happy.

HAPPY: I'm not a pansy, Fuller. You have compassion for the wrong assholes.

FULLER: How do you know?

HAPPY: When we go to parties together, I see how you act. You go soft and tender. I read people well. Some people have this gift. I'm shrewder than you.

FULLER: I have a conscience, Happy.

HAPPY: So do I. Don't get lofty, asshole. Sometimes you have to choose between patriotism and conscience. I don't mean to insult you. Let's toughen up.

FULLER: Do me a favor. Take my man. Celebrity swap.

HAPPY: The Jew?

FULLER: I'll cover Cortez.

HAPPY: Want me to be your point man?

FULLER: Aguneir won't break. Not with me. Sweet talk an Israeli? Don't know what button to push. Cortez is more my style. I'll owe you one, Happy.

HAPPY: Tickets to the Garden?

FULLER: Alright.

HAPPY: These twits are all the same to me. We chop them down and ship them out. It's a deal. *(They nod to each other.* HAPPY *lights cigarette, then discards it.)* My wife ran away last night, Fuller. She's seeing somebody while I work late. I give her my checks. I never ask for anything in return. I went shopping for her. What a cunt. Has my mind all bent out. Tells me I'm in metabolic decline. Mr. Rust. What's a guy to do, Fuller? I'm young and well hung. With a little help, I can get it up. If this continues, I plan to kill the little missus. I'll staple her head to our wedding album. You know the feeling, man? When the audacity cuts through your heart with the coldest blade. The asinine smile of deceit in her eyes. I give her one last chance. I can be liberal, Fuller. I still love her madly. *(Pause)* Your wife is faithful.

FULLER: Yeah.

HAPPY: How come?

FULLER: I go home early and take care of business. Attentiveness. Magic word. *(Pause)* Give it time, Happy. What the hell happened to your ears?

HAPPY: *(Pointing to tape marks along his earlobes)* These? Acupuncture.

FULLER: For what?

HAPPY: Therapy.

FULLER: Therapy?

HAPPY: For impotence. *(Laughs)* For smoking. Trying to kick it altogether. Almost burned myself in bed last week.

FULLER: Is it working?

HAPPY: *(Demonstrating)* You got to rub them every once in a while. Whenever the urge comes. Stimulates the nerves. I feel a change. Makes me civil. I don't smoke much around here. I just rub my Goddamn ears.

FULLER: And it makes you happy?

HAPPY: Who the fuck knows.

FULLER: Take the Israeli, Happy. He's a madman. You're the pro. Give me the keys to your girlfriend's room. I'll see Miss Cortez. *(HAPPY tosses keys to FULLER.)*

SCENE SIX

(Later that day: AGUNEIR's room)

AGUNEIR: Who the hell are you?

HAPPY: Agent Logan, United States Immigration.

AGUNEIR: Where's the other idiot?

HAPPY: Re-assignment.

AGUNEIR: What are you, the designated hitter?

HAPPY: I'm here to make you more comfortable.

AGUNEIR: I want color television and a Jacuzzi. Quick, yo-yo.

HAPPY: Anything else?

AGUNEIR: I want my insulin.

HAPPY: No more insulin. Drug store just closed.

AGUNEIR: Listen, I'm not a young man like yourself. I can't tolerate these clubhouse games. The colored man didn't like me. You won't either.

HAPPY: You had asked for his supervisor.

AGUNEIR: I'm to have insulin every morning. Clean food. And I want my personal things back. I pray each morning with my prayer book and shawl.

HAPPY: A vegetarian lives longer, has finer bowel movements, and maintains a superior memory. Are you a vegetarian? *(Pause)* Why do you pray? Tell me, I'm curious. When you carry such hatred, how do you expect God to hear your prayers?

AGUNEIR: Because my prayers have passion.

HAPPY: And so do mine. And I pray all the time. For peace in this world. I pray for all the world's children. Yours and mine. I'm a spiritual person, even as I work for the government. And I'm a happy spirit. We need more happy spirits. Why not be one? *(Pause)* Talk to me. I know nothing about you. What is Judaism? Or militancy? You're not a typical Jew. You've got a set of balls. *(Pause)* There was another bombing last night.

AGUNEIR: I know nothing about it.

HAPPY: A small Arab child is now in critical condition at the hospital.

AGUNEIR: I'm very sorry.

HAPPY: Are you?

AGUNEIR: I am.

HAPPY: I don't believe you.

AGUNEIR: Believe what you want.

HAPPY: Agent Fuller — the colored man — was exceptionally kind to you.

AGUNEIR: In this world, one can never be too kind.

HAPPY: How kind should I be?

AGUNEIR: Give me my insulin. *(Pause)* I know who you are. I know.

HAPPY: I'm going to crack your skull like a walnut, Rabbi.

AGUNEIR: *(Indifferent; removes tobacco)* Cigarette?

HAPPY: I'm trying to quit.

AGUNEIR: Menthol. Won't kill you.

HAPPY: *(Snatches it from* AGUNEIR's mouth) Eat the cigarette.

AGUNEIR: *(Removes second cigarette)* Mr. Logan, you're dealing with an elected member of the Israeli Knesset. A political dignitary. Surely, you've reached puberty? (HAPPY snatches cigarette.) I sense you don't respect me.

HAPPY: I hate Jews like you.

AGUNEIR: What are we going to do about that?

HAPPY: I want the fucking bombings to stop.

AGUNEIR: Didn't the colored man tell you I don't squeal? I hold up very well. You won't. I know you. Is it money that you want? How much, Mr. Logan? I'll lubricate you.

HAPPY: How much?

AGUNEIR: Rich man I'm not. But name an amount. This I did not offer the other agent. Tell me your price.

HAPPY: Fifty thousand.

AGUNEIR: Alright.

HAPPY: How would I get it?

AGUNEIR: From my bank in Manhattan.

HAPPY: I can't go to a bank.

AGUNEIR: I'm not free to get it, Mr. Logan.

HAPPY: Ask someone to go for you. And have them come here.

AGUNEIR: Perhaps.

HAPPY: Give me his name.

AGUNEIR: I can't. It's too dangerous.

HAPPY: Deal's off.

AGUNEIR: You talk to me like I work in the garment district. We must be discreet, Mr. Logan, lest we risk a misunderstanding.

HAPPY: What is his name?

AGUNEIR: His name is Ed.

HAPPY: Ed what?

AGUNEIR: The comic. Ed Koch. I can vouch for him.

HAPPY: (Grabs AGUNEIR's lapels) Don't jerk me around, Aguneir!

AGUNEIR: Let go of me.

HAPPY: (Slaps AGUNEIR) Time's running out.

AGUNEIR: You're worse than the colored man. He had manners.

HAPPY: (Menacing) I have manners. You're going to see my manners.

AGUNEIR: (Calmly) Drop dead, Mr. Logan.

HAPPY: Deep down, every Jew's a villian. Born an American. Military service. University degrees. You leave your native country. Dubious Zionistic goals. A racist. Your file shows a history of mental instability. Do you talk to yourself when left alone?

AGUNEIR: I'm talking to myself right now.

HAPPY: You know me.

AGUNEIR: Yes.

HAPPY: Then be afraid of me. I've a very short fuse.

AGUNEIR: Do you?

HAPPY: You shoot Arabs.

AGUNEIR: Nonsense.

HAPPY: (Pulling AGUNEIR's hair back) Answer me.

AGUNEIR: No.

HAPPY: You have no moral conscience. (Pushing AGUNEIR's head to one side)

AGUNEIR: *(Recovering)* Mr. Logan, what is the point of these brilliant questions? *(Pause)* You bore me. The interrogation's over.

HAPPY: If there is one more bombing, I'm going to scramble your brains with a wooden spoon.

AGUNEIR: How can I stop the bombings?

HAPPY: Pray. Nod your ugly Yiddish head and pray. I'm not the colored man. You damn well better pray.

SCENE SEVEN

(Fourth day: CORTEZ's *room)*

CORTEZ: I'm quite ill.

FULLER: I know.

CORTEZ: I've diarrhea. Fever. Spasms.

FULLER: We gave it to you. In the food. Salmonella. *(Pause)* If you'd like, we can get you a medic.

CORTEZ: Yes.

FULLER: All our medics are good.

CORTEZ: I'm sure.

FULLER: This is as far as I'll push you. I've read your list of names. They read more or less complete.

CORTEZ: Logan appeared satisfied.

FULLER: Yes. We play good cop, bad cop routines.

CORTEZ: Which cop are you?

FULLER: The good cop.

CORTEZ: Is it that you want names, or the sheer satisfaction of seeing my corporal body contorted? You've made me sick and weak. Resorting to food poison. If you have any decency...use physical force. Is it because I am a woman?

FULLER: Everything's a factor.

CORTEZ: Your partner's not very bright. You seem more refined.

FULLER: Do I?

CORTEZ: You're a cautious man, Mr. Fuller. I see it in your countenance. I see your crude strategies on your face. Perhaps it's because I have severe cramps and delirium. In jail, many things are possible. One either finds renewed strength or weakness. Did I seem easy to you?

FULLER: No.

CORTEZ: Did I do so much to merit this descent? Was it a sneer? A mischosen word in some obscure newspaper? Well, well, well, my diarrhea speaks to me most eloquently. Mr. Fuller, if you were me...and I you...would depression set in? Despondency? Would you cave in? Write tawdry poems of despair on the prison walls? Imagine a B-movie based on your squalor.

FULLER: Consider yourself lucky.

CORTEZ: You let them exploit you.

FULLER: I'm doing my job.

CORTEZ: And you fed shit to Angelica?

FULLER: I'm not allowed to say.

CORTEZ: Your sympathies are for the wrong people. Whom do you have locked up next door?

FULLER: An Israeli.

CORTEZ: I can hear him at night, screaming madly. Crying like a child. What's in his bowels? Are you beating the daylights out of him?

FULLER: No one's beating him.

CORTEZ: I think you're beating him around the clock. Is it like Argentina in the 70s? Are you beating him with American magazines?

FULLER: Israelis are remarkable tough creatures.

CORTEZ: What prevented my own beatings, Mr. Fuller?

FULLER: I stepped in.

CORTEZ: Should I believe you?

FULLER: You gave us significant information.

CORTEZ: I gave you names of little consequence. Names you never needed. I'm very ill, Mr. Fuller. I hate to mess. Where is this indispensible medic?

FULLER: Somewhere in the building.

CORTEZ: The names I gave you...I regret. You will get no more names. How wretched I feel. For being civil with you. My fever rises. Did you feed me cat's piss? Your mother's cooking? I don't understand your country. Last year I arrived in New York without incident. I don't understand the paranoia. What a mystery it is. I have a sister here, in Boston. Well, you know this. She knows this country. Is not shocked by it. It may be cultural. It may be utter capriciousness. Mr. Fuller, you people have fortified my passions. My mind has formed certain blisters. In time they will burst. Mr. Fuller, I need the bathroom now. Unlock the door. A spasm of stomach pain. *(Pause)* You have to open the door for me. *(*FULLER *rises.)* Such chivalry. You are a gentleman.

SCENE EIGHT

(Later that day: Lounge)

FULLER: What the hell are you doing?

HAPPY: *(Rolling marijuana)* Coffee break. Hell of a day, Fuller. The claustrophobia gets out of hand. Need a window. A little weed, medicinal. Like tea to the English. Subliminal. Transcendental. The home remedies we seek. *(Lights up)* We're not on Earth to suffer. There's no point to pain. That's why I come home late each night. Long strolls at the mall. A toke. It's my beatific marriage. She stays in the bathroom for hours. The neurotic accusations. The price we pay for working late, for eating alone, for combing the house for clues, for masturbating while she sleeps. The long days without gratification. There must be an escape.

FULLER: Trout fishing.

HAPPY: What?

FULLER: Fishing is very calm. Quiet rivers. Natural sounds. The flight of birds.

HAPPY: Too fucking dull, Fuller. I need tumult. Bam, bam, bam. Aqueduct and the Flats. OTB. Fucking action. Hot winners. Talking dirty to a ditsy blonde at the track. Wrapping her thighs around the broadest smile on Earth. Drinking life. Fishing? Hell, Fuller, I'm a scuba diver. *(Extending cigarette to* FULLER*)* A toke, Mr. Straight?

FULLER: No.

HAPPY: Don't judge me, Fuller. I'm going through a period of tension.

FULLER: I don't judge people, man.

HAPPY: How's my Spanish girlfriend?

FULLER: Recovering, though the diarrhea's still severe.

HAPPY: Medic came?

FULLER: An hour ago.

HAPPY: She'll drop a couple of pounds. She'll thank us.

FULLER: I think we pissed her off.

HAPPY: We broke her like a house puppy. She cowered to us. Sends one on the grandest ego trip.

FULLER: Not me.

HAPPY: You get off on it, Fuller. I've seen it. *(Pause)* Because you're just like me. We're the same shit. *(Pause)* When I get stoned, Fuller, I feel all the Goddamn wrinkles fall out. I feel freedom, love for humanity. I think about the glorious 60s. The flowers and simple pink nudity. Big fucking tits and gorgeous sun flowers with Van Gogh and Jimi Hendrix. A return trip from Saigon. *(Pause)* Come, take a hit. *(Pause)* I would hate to be locked in this jail, Fuller. Makes me fucking blue. No clocks. No vents. The fucking odors here. The hidden mikes behind the corrugated ceiling tile. Polygraphs up the ass. Telegrams from Washington pushing for speed. Pushing us harder. Just pushing too far. The mind is a complicated lock. So fucking hard to pick. Everyone's picking someone's brains. *(Pause)* Cortez is such a Latin cocktease. Her black pantyhose, Fuller. You know what I mean.

FULLER: You're falling in love with her, shithead.

HAPPY: Can you tell?

FULLER: I know you very well.

HAPPY: We spent a few years together.

FULLER: A few years.

HAPPY: We're a team, buddy. A terrific fucking team.

FULLER: Go easy on that stuff.

HAPPY: The Israeli is fucking us up. We finish him off now. He's not getting his insulin. I've made a switch.

FULLER: On whose authority?

HAPPY: My own.

FULLER: I don't know, Happy.

HAPPY: I've twenty-four hours to deadline.

FULLER: Do you want to team up on him? You look wiped out.

HAPPY: No, I'm staying all night, Fuller.

FULLER: Why?

HAPPY: To surprise the ballbusting Jew. It's got to happen by tonight.

FULLER: Don't go overboard. You're putting in too many hours.

HAPPY: I've got fucking stamina.

FULLER: Stamina for what?

HAPPY: Stamina to mount the head of this militant Jew. Not because he's a mad zealot. Not because he plays us for little idiots. I do it for kicks. A sport. I am the watchdog for Liberty.

FULLER: Your eyes are so fucking bloodshot. You look like shit.

HAPPY: I'm going to crack him tonight. My honor. I won't sleep. Going to teach him the waltz and sweep the cell clean. *(Pause)* Submission. *(Pause)* And then I'll celebrate with Miss Latin American. Party time. Come on, Fuller, doesn't she turn you on?

FULLER: Go home.

HAPPY: No.

FULLER: Go home, Happy.

HAPPY: Fuller... *(Steady eye contact; in a moment)* I can't. There's someone with Joyce tonight.

FULLER: How do you know?

HAPPY: I heard on the extension phone.

FULLER: I'm sorry.

HAPPY: I'd go home to break his goddamn neck, but the asshole's 6'2" and an amateur boxer. I'm not looking for humiliation in my fucking living room. My home life is down the tubes. *(Pause)* Get the fuck out of here, Fuller.

SCENE NINE

(Fifth day: AGUNEIR's *room.* AGUNEIR's *face is severely bruised.)*

FULLER: Are you alright? I can call the medic. We have pain killers. *(Pause)* My partner was under pressure. One too many bombings. He means well. I'm very sorry for what happened. I guarantee you, it won't happen again.

AGUNEIR: Go to hell.

FULLER: He simply ran out of time. His methods are not my methods. I should have stayed with you last night. I could have guessed this. *(Offers cigarette to* AGUNEIR, *who accepts)* Agent Logan completed your release forms. Apparently, you played ball with him. I'm very glad. As soon as your face heals, we're going to fly you back to Jerusalem. Obviously, you can't remain in the States. *(Pause)* They tell me vitamin E is good for skin wounds. Would you like to try some? *(Produces vial of tablets)* Well, I'll leave them with you. Agent Logan has turned you over to me for the duration of your stay. Naturally, I will do everything I can to make you feel comfortable. Our job is done. Except for the formalities. *(Pause)* Is there anything I can do for you, Mr. Aguneir? Mr. Aguneir?

AGUNEIR: I want to leave now.

FULLER: But your face...

AGUNEIR: I'll wear sunglasses.

FULLER: We can't allow that.

AGUNEIR: Then get the hell out of my sight.

FULLER: I never meant you any harm.

AGUNEIR: What he did to me, you are an accomplice. In God's eyes. In my eyes.

FULLER: I meant you no harm.

AGUNEIR: Only the finest hospitality. Last night was my Sabbath. You violated my Sabbath. You've desecrated my own person. You spit on my soul. Get out of here. Logan stole my medicine. You rupture me with total contempt. What are you looking at? Get out of here! I gave you information. So get out of here. I was born in this country. I fought in Korea. And you shit on me. Get out, Fuller. I can't urinate.

FULLER: I'll send in the medic.

AGUNEIR: Send in a rabbi. (Pause) You heard me. (Pause) You must relish my humiliation.

FULLER: No.

AGUNEIR: My bedsheets are soiled.

FULLER: I'll have them changed.

AGUNEIR: Am I to believe that you're the moderate among the American Nazis? You practice no restraints? Logan is your superior?

FULLER: Yes.

AGUNEIR: And he does what he wants?

FULLER: Within limits.

AGUNEIR: And you say nothing about it?

FULLER: What should I say?

AGUNEIR: Each man owns a conscience.

FULLER: Yes.

AGUNEIR: For a colored man, you're quite accommodating. You should be sensitive to human rights. Not compromising what you hold as common decency. But you get by. You survive, tail between your legs. Pathetic. Logan is a monster. Your half-wit superior. He makes hideous racial jokes about you. Yes. I find it very offensive.

FULLER: He bad mouths for a reason.

AGUNEIR: What's the reason?

FULLER: He flies off the handle, that's all.

AGUNEIR: I don't like nigger jokes, Mr. Fuller. Believe what you want. I tell you, your colleague's a racist and a demon.

FULLER: And what are you?

AGUNEIR: I am now crippled.

FULLER: Nonsense.

AGUNEIR: Fuck you. (Pause) I am a separatist. There are nations which must house minorities. There are nations which dominate minorities. This is not the time to instruct you, Mr. Fuller, about the Diaspora. But the Bible says I am right. So I am a separatist. By necessity. Every government in history has punished my people. My world stands apart from others. And I'm outspoken about it. Colored people have suffered too. So you know the deeper truths. Yes? A man like Logan knifes you in the back. I don't. Which do you prefer? (Pause) What sort of friendship have you with him? He cares for you like a Bircher. Like a lyncher. Like the hooded figure behind a gasoline cross. You are a colossal fool.

FULLER: I'll get the medic.

AGUNEIR: Ask him. Go see. Get burned. Burn him.

FULLER: You're delirious.

AGUNEIR: I speak the truth. You cannot be coy about a hatred. What happens when a black nationalist comes to New York? Do you drag him here? Do you take liberties? Beat him senseless? Do you draw straws for each turn?

FULLER: Conserve your strength.

AGUNEIR: You and your partner belong in the Middle Ages during the Holy Terror. God will foil you when a sudden fright jumps out of your skin.

FULLER: My job's important to me. I take it quite seriously. We provide a necessary service to national security. Rude as it might seem to you.

AGUNEIR: I think you're full of shit.

FULLER: You're entitled to think what you want.

AGUNEIR: I think persecuted people should carry guns under their jackets and shoot without hesitation all government officials. I think your magnificent xenophobia has exceeded all thresholds. I think you and your squinty-eyed partner will live forever in this pig dungeon. I think you know the depth of my recalcitrant feelings.

FULLER: Yes, I think I do. *(Pause)* You're turning color.

AGUNEIR: No matter how badly you paint me, and curse me, I have sovereignty over my life and well being. Bandages and all. There is a sick man in this cot. I will nail your partner, Mr. Fuller. I swear to you, as God is my witness, I will. I will make him swallow his wicked little tongue. He will choke. Now fetch your Goddamn medic before I explode inside.

SCENE TEN

(Continuation, Day Five: CORTEZ's *room)*

HAPPY: You're leaving us, Miss Cortez. I'm so glad to give you the news. A little smile for the gentleman? *(Pause)* You've lost weight, I see. Aged. What a woman loses in beauty, she gains in character. How good to release you in time for the holiday weekend. I personally thank you for assisting our investigation. Some of your information was invaluable to our work. In the short time we became acquainted, I grew to understand your politics, your diction, your perfume, and your unique personal struggles. *(Pause)* I was moved, Miss Cortez. How rare that is. And how strange to be telling you this. To trust you at this stage. To feel tenderness. *(Pause)* Any questions?

CORTEZ: Where do I go?

HAPPY: Back to Colombia, of course.

CORTEZ: I've seen the morning newspapers.

HAPPY: Yes?

CORTEZ: Your Under-Secretary of State has branded me in the blackest of colors. You know I risk reprisals in my city from this adverse publicity.

HAPPY: Oh, come now, Miss Cortez...

CORTEZ: There are midnight death squads, Mr. Logan, funded by the right.

HAPPY: That's not our problem.

CORTEZ: This was your plan. Make me even more odious to the far right.

HAPPY: I don't play politics, Miss Cortez. I wouldn't dream of playing with your life.

CORTEZ: I can be either a martyr or an emigre'. Thank you. Colombia, you have taken away.

HAPPY: Denmark's a lovely place. Or New Zealand. I know a terrific travel agent. So many places to go, Miss Cortez. The world's at your feet.

CORTEZ: Stop conning me.

HAPPY: You're right. I am conning you. How low of me. *(Pause)* I apologize for the dysentery. As gentlemen, we tried to meet you halfway. Please believe this. Here, government is striving for some aspect of perfection. I came to accept your convictions. You've something which I envy.

CORTEZ: Pray tell, what?

HAPPY: Intellectual dedication.

CORTEZ: Am I to believe you?

HAPPY: Yes. Particularly because you're a sexual woman. I mean, the hot motor is working. I hear sizzling Latin rhythms. I hear love singing. You're a formidable individual, Miss Cortez. And I admire the roundness of your breasts. Your beautiful rosewater lips. Why should I be shy? Perhaps we could have dinner? *(Pause)* Tomorrow we take you to the airport.

CORTEZ: And you're going to miss me?

HAPPY: Yes.

CORTEZ: Isn't that a wedding ring?

HAPPY: It was.

CORTEZ: Who taught you the art of flirting, Mr. Logan?

HAPPY: American instinct.

CORTEZ: I see. *(Pause)* Cultivate your chastity, Mr. Logan. So when your princess comes, she'll be able to admire you. *(Silence)* Will there be a press conference at the airport?

HAPPY: No.

CORTEZ: And if I'm recognized at the airport by reporters?

HAPPY: You'll wear a disguise. A funny-looking Stetson. A black veil. The best disguise is a subjective manner. Just be demure, Miss Cortez.

CORTEZ: And what has happened to Angelica?

HAPPY: She was released the day before.

CORTEZ: Did you molest her?

HAPPY: Did we molest you?

CORTEZ: She passed me a note, Mr. Logan.

HAPPY: And did you pass her a note?

CORTEZ: She and I will remember this incident for a very long time. I will empty myself of it.

HAPPY: Be my guest.

CORTEZ: I will portray you.

HAPPY: How so?

CORTEZ: Emblematically. On all fours.

HAPPY: As you wish. Here's your travel prescription. *(Hands over pills for dysentery)* Won't you have dinner with me?

CORTEZ: How kind of you, Mr. Logan. You show a side of civility so late in the day. Could it be that a gentleman hides inside? The ugly troll under the toll bridge. A political Rumpelstilskin. I came for a literary award but leave with the anger of a rape victim. Am I really more dangerous than you, Mr. Logan?

HAPPY: Yes. Your language, Miss Cortez. It's your language.

CORTEZ: And if we had met at a bar, under different circumstances...

HAPPY: Are you making a pass at me, Miss Cortez?

CORTEZ: Of course. Can't you tell?

HAPPY: I understand your human needs. Perhaps a good man between your legs would vivify you?

CORTEZ: What a mature thing to say. You put love so delicately.

HAPPY: *(Falsely flattered)* Thank you.

CORTEZ: The inferior male hormones in your blood, Mr. Logan, have set you back a thousand years. You need a shot of estrogen and a large dose of rationality. Shout your mother's name when you reach your final coronary. You have no savior. How I pity you.

SCENE ELEVEN

(Day Six: Lounge)

FULLER: He came in this morning without calling.

HAPPY: Where was I?

FULLER: I don't know. He went over the files. Checked the paper shredder. Asked a lot of questions.

HAPPY: What's his name?

FULLER: Monteith.

HAPPY: The Under-Secretary?

FULLER: Yes.

HAPPY: Did he say when he was coming back?

FULLER: No. Happy, he's a real snoop.

HAPPY: Did he visit the rooms?

FULLER: Yes. Ward B.

HAPPY: The Israeli's?

FULLER: Yes.

HAPPY: Why the hell didn't you detour him?

FULLER: He's a charging bull.

HAPPY: Shit, shit, shit. I've got to make a dozen phone calls. You really blew it, Fuller.

FULLER: Hell, Monteith's got top clearance.

HAPPY: Smarts, Fuller...this is the beginning of a set-up. Can't you smell it? Did he speak with the detainees?

FULLER: Yeah.

HAPPY: Someone blew the whistle on us.

FULLER: Why?

HAPPY: Because the wheel turns.

FULLER: Who?

HAPPY: An insider. Maybe a medic. Or food services. Shit. We should clean house now. These guys will stop at nothing. Countermanding the last eighteen months of bonuses. Just when we were rolling.

FULLER: Aguneir's bruises are outrageous, Happy.

HAPPY: Did he speak to Monteith?

FULLER: No.

HAPPY: Out he goes. Call the garage. Get a driver ready. And flight arrangements. Did Monteith take photos?

FULLER: Yes.

HAPPY: We're fucked! They're going to ream us! Of all times for an on-site. Shit, shit, shit! Give me the keys to Aguneir's room.

FULLER: The damage is done.

HAPPY: Give me the fucking keys.

FULLER: *(Tossing keys)* I thought you were on good terms with the brass.

HAPPY: So did I.

FULLER: Don't do anything rash, Happy.

HAPPY: They're looking for a scapegoat. Traffic light just changed color in Washington. This building was off limits to Congress. State was supposed to protect us. We have to cover our asses now. Such bastards at State. You'd think after cracking two headliners, they'd throw us a bone. I'm going to name Delancy and his teammates. Such fucking bastards in Washington. We can fix it. Enough belly aching. I'm getting rid of the Jew.

SCENE TWELVE

(Continuation, as if MONTEITH *is already present. Lounge. Day Six.)*

MONTEITH: Are you Mr. Logan?

HAPPY: Yes.

MONTEITH: Agent Fuller has discussed the events of the last two weeks with me. Is there anything you care to say with regard to his statement?

HAPPY: You issued a report, Fuller?

FULLER: *(Reluctantly)* No.

MONTEITH: Mr. Logan, this is an informal investigation.

HAPPY: Don't railroad me with games about procedure.

MONTEITH: You've a bright set of brass balls, Mr. Logan. Don't dismiss the gross irregularities here. And wipe that smirk off your face.

HAPPY: I'm not responsible for health problems within this building.

MONTEITH: I think you are. And your associate. Ward B's like a chamber of horrors.

HAPPY: You guys structured Ward B. We're just following established policy.

MONTEITH: I don't think so, Mr. Logan.

HAPPY: Are you bringing us up for charges?

MONTEITH: *(Nonchalant)* I'm going to hang you out to dry, yes.

HAPPY: You knew he was a diabetic. *(Pause)* We had requests from your channels to detain him, to uncover his links with the terrorists in New York. I have letters saying so. And I can release these letters to the press. *(Pause)* Think about it. I've no loyalty to Delancy and his team.

MONTEITH: Mr. Logan, Chaim Aguneir is in critical condition. Ostensibly, from a massive stroke. The timing couldn't be worse. The lacerations to his face and upper chest are simply astounding. Don't ask me to believe this came from a fall in the shower. If either one of you induced this problem...well, the Devil has joined our little coterie at Immigration Services. If you lie to me, I promise to be double punitive. You can bet your pensions on that.

FULLER: We were working under extreme pressure, brought on by your people. You know our ways.

MONTEITH: I didn't come here to hand out citations for valor, Mr. Fuller. Don't tell me dirty business was sanctioned by a Washington bureau. But if you reveal, to the best of your knowledge, who ordered the Israeli's beating and which of you complied with that order...it would make my visit that much simpler. Tell me who withheld his insulin...who extorted compliance from the medics with the insulin substitute...who assumed the freedom to play Almighty God, gentlemen. *(Pause)* If the Israeli comes out of his stroke, I can circumvent this interview. I'm a pessimist by nature. *(Pause)* Gentlemen, now's the time to sing. *(Pause)* The young woman Cortez is free to meet a death squad outside her home in Bogota. Stunning work, gentlemen.

FULLER: We were just following your office's line.

HAPPY: We never went to the press. You guys did.

MONTEITH: The momentum started here. Under your nose. You should have just sent the woman back on the next plane. Yes, gentlemen. So, no more snivelling. You can incriminate yourselves, or each other. I don't really care. Just don't waste my time.

HAPPY: Who sent you? *(Pause)* I would like advice from counsel, Mr. Monteith.

MONTEITH: I'm sorry, Mr. Logan, but we will carry on as though marooned far away from civilization. We can pretend behind closed doors. Tell each other stories. Perhaps strike a deal.

HAPPY: What sort of deal?

MONTEITH: A deal of mutual convenience.

FULLER: For whom?

MONTEITH: For our warm little family.

FULLER: *(After a beat)* Alright.

MONTEITH: Mr. Logan?

HAPPY: I need to think it over.

MONTEITH: *(After a beat)* Mr. Logan?

HAPPY: Alright.

MONTEITH: Mr. Logan, were you assigned Chaim Aguneir?

HAPPY: What difference does it make? *(Pause)* I interceded with Aguneir's interrogation. Fuller had trouble.

MONTEITH: Mr. Fuller, do you know if Mr. Logan used excessive physical punishment during the interrogation?

FULLER: No.

MONTEITH: But you were aware of Chaim Aguneir's condition?

FULLER: Only what you yourself know.

MONTEITH: Is Mr. Logan a sadist?

FULLER: I don't think so.

MONTEITH: Do you think we should employ sadists in this department?

HAPPY: Now just a second, damnit...

MONTEITH: *(Ignoring* HAPPY*)* Mr. Fuller, on occasion the branches of government conflict with one another. Was your department issued a memorandum from another agency?

FULLER: Mr. Logan receives all memorandums.

MONTEITH: Can you name someone above Mr. Logan who may have issued any orders to play hard ball with a detainee? *(Silence)* Mr. Logan, were there any memorandums about this?

HAPPY: Regarding Cortez from Colombia, yes.

MONTEITH: Can I see this memorandum?

HAPPY: Only telephone confirmation.

MONTEITH: Saying what?

HAPPY: You know the wording.

MONTEITH: Be explicit, Mr. Logan, lest I risk a misunderstanding.

HAPPY: Mr. Monteith, I'm not a rookie at this sort of thing. I like my department. Have pride in my work. Your questions are demoralizing.

MONTEITH: I'm very sorry, Mr. Logan.

HAPPY: We do a very good job at Immigration.

MONTEITH: Yes, I know.

HAPPY: You send us lists of undesirables. You request intelligence information. We obey. It's a little hypocritical, Mr. Monteith — Sir — to expect us to play clean with your dirty favors. You're here because you need a fall guy. *(Pause)* I really wish I knew who sent you. It's a bit disheartening to feel like a political stooge. Don't I have intrinsic worth? It's true about the Israeli. Orders were to detain him. To fucking crack him. Quickly. There was danger in New York. A shitload of bombings. His arrogance was too rich for my blood, Mr. Monteith. I found I hated things about him. His demoniacal bullshit. I'm not a fucking anti-Semite. We need Jews in the world. But it's very hard to like an uppity Jew, like Chaim Aguneir. Arab racist, pure and simple. Well, be glad that I cracked the son-of-a-bitch. A menace to our society. It makes me very happy to serve Immigration. *(Pause)* Of course, you want to go about this with white gloves and an angel's halo. We're not fucking pansies here, Mr. Monteith. We're patriotic, hard-working family men in a thankless role. Working in twilight so you pretty boys can look good. So I advise you to return to your particular branch up there in the fucking stratosphere and convey my profound regrets over the Israeli's untimely stroke. *(Pause)* And, should he drop dead in the hospital, we can shed crocodile tears and consider ourselves lucky for a time.

MONTEITH: For your sake, pray that he comes through. Do you understand? I will take a life for a life.

FULLER: We will pray.

MONTEITH: Perhaps at this point I might do better talking with you alone.

HAPPY: There's no need to. Fuller and I are very close.

MONTEITH: Mr. Logan, would you excuse us...please?

HAPPY: You're not going to play us against each other. Don't waste your time. I won't say a word against Fuller. He's like a brother. And he'll say the same.

MONTEITH: Mr. Logan, I'll be with you shortly. Please don't hold up this review.

HAPPY: Fuller, do we have a pact?

FULLER: Yeah.

HAPPY: You mean it.

FULLER: Yeah.

HAPPY: We're together forever?

FULLER: Yeah, Happy.

HAPPY: God bless you, Fuller. You're the man of the hour.

MONTEITH: Get lost, Mr. Logan. I'll call you when I need you.

SCENE THIRTEEN

(Day Six, continued)

MONTEITH: Mr. Fuller, I'm about to tell you the fable of the fox and the cocker spaniel. *(Pause)* There was once a farm with the kindest family around. And on this wonderful farm were all sorts of livestock who lived very wonderful lives. They had sheep and cows and ducks and pigs and, of course, a hen house. The family kept the farm in order with their trusty cocker spaniel. Whenever there was any trouble, the cocker spaniel would bark and warn the family. One day, a fox snuck into the farm and passed itself off as one of the farm goats. Everyone was fooled but the cocker spaniel. The cocker spaniel had keen sense, Mr. Fuller. *(Pause)* If you've heard this story before, I'll stop....*(Pause)* So the spaniel approached the fox one day and let him know that not everyone was fooled. But the fox was clever and spoke back: "Hey, I'm just like you...in need of a good home. I promise not to do any harm. Just treat me like one of the gang." *(Pause)* Now the spaniel felt in his bones that this was wrong, but just could not find the anger to bark at this tricky little fox. Then, some weeks later, the hens were attacked by the fox. *(Pause)* Now the family rounded up all the animals that day and asked them what they knew. And you know what? The fox whispered to the spaniel, "Don't be pernicious." *(Pause)* Mr. Fuller, do you know the meaning of pernicious? *(Pause)* It is sinful to be pernicious. Don't put the family in peril...I want to talk to you about loyalty, Mr. Fuller. When I was in grad school, for pleasure I read Hegel. You would benefit by his wisdom. You have ties with friends and family. You have responsibility to yourself. You have allegiance to the State. Whenever there is a conflict with these three categories, Mr. Fuller, which do you choose? *(Pause)* Mr. Fuller, the irregularities and criminal proceedings in this detention center astound one. I'm giving you a chance to save your own neck. I must turn someone in. If I must, all of you will be indicted. Make my case easier, and you can keep your job. *(Pause)* Well, I'm going to leave a pencil and legal pad for you to write a deposition on your superior, Mr. Logan. Be truthful and merciless, Mr. Fuller, because in this business there are no loyalties.

SCENE FOURTEEN

(Day Seven: Lounge)

MONTEITH: Sit down, Mr. Logan. *(Pause)* Agent Fuller's deposition was completed yesterday.

HAPPY: Is it consistent with mine?

MONTEITH: No.

HAPPY: Serious discrepancies?

MONTEITH: Yes.

HAPPY: What exactly did Fuller say?

MONTEITH: That you brutalized Chaim Aguneir with a rubber hose. (HAPPY *tries to interrupt.*) And that your attack contributed to his stroke.

HAPPY: It's not true.

MONTEITH: Mr. Logan, it would help your case considerably if you changed your own statement. *(Pause)* Mr. Logan, I understand you have a daughter.

HAPPY: Yes?

MONTEITH: How old is she?

HAPPY: Almost six.

MONTEITH: Do you love her?

HAPPY: Indeed I do.

MONTEITH: What is her name?

HAPPY: Ginger.

MONTEITH: Do you want good things for your little girl?

HAPPY: Of course.

MONTEITH: I have a little girl too. Her name is Suzy. She can steal
your heart so tenderly. Daddy...Daddy...Daddy...look what
fatherhood does to a man....*(Pause)* Mr. Logan, why not speak the
truth? We could close this investigation that much sooner. Do it for
Ginger. *(Pause)* I look at your face, Mr. Logan, and my heart goes out
to you. I see guilt, contortion, sorrow. Such a dreadful sight. I see
tremendous sickness and pain in your leathered face. Make a full
admission. Clear your conscience. How will you ever find peace in
your present state? *(Pause)* Cigarette? Coffee? *(Pause)* Mr. Logan...I
want to tell you about the extraordinary fable of the errant church
mouse and the sacred wine cellar. Yes, there in the hidden chambers
of a lovely country church, lived a meek and lonely church mouse.
The church mouse cooked and cleaned and was generally an
upstanding inhabitant of the church community. But it came to pass
that the church mouse discovered the sacred wine of old in the
church cellar. At first the mouse refused to open the wine. But, after a
time, the mouse-with-some-cheek began to use teaspoons of wine for
cooking. And regrettably, the mouse began to drink directly from the
wine bottles. His deviant behavior eventually gave him away.
Slurred speech, aggressive, a little red nose. A drunk is a drunk.
(Pause) Have you heard this story, Mr. Logan? It's a very old story.
(Pause) The community recognized his sickness and his unmitigated
sadness. He was after all a disgusting alcoholic church mouse.
Prematurely wizened. So hideous to the community. He would
receive his just punishment. For, secretly, the mouse yearned for his
vindication. For, secretly, we all yearn for vindication. How many
bridges must we cross, Mr. Logan? I see your pockmarked skin
turning color. Release yourself. I promise not to abuse you. Say how
you picked up the weapon, and how many times you struck the
Israeli. Tell me what was in your tormented mind during the attack.

All I ask is for details. Mr. Logan, was it better than any activity in bed? *(Pause)* Mr. Logan, pick up the pencil and write. The community will support you. You are a wounded bird in need of a milk tit. A new world awaits you. *(After a pause)* Your friend can rest easy now that you will come to his aid. I want you to tell him that. He'll be here shortly. It will be your honesty, Mr. Logan, which will impress him the most. And your new-found grace. May you find a bit of peace in your heart. Write.

HAPPY: *(Slowly picking up pencil; unable to write)* And how is Aguneir?

MONTEITH: He died this morning.

HAPPY: Then whatever I write won't matter. You have Fuller's testimony.

MONTEITH: *(Fatherly)* Put it down on paper, Mr. Logan. Word for word. It will be for your benefit alone. *(Exits)*

SCENE FIFTEEN

(Continuation of Scene Fourteen: Change of light.)

HAPPY: *(To MONTEITH's chair)* Pride makes me vain. Love has deserted me. And this unsightly twist in my glorious career, at the worst possible time...who cursed me? I love my country. I so do love my country. Aguneir, I have made countless sacrifices to my beloved country. My country means everything to me. Like all the stars in the sky. Dear God in Heaven, give me back my country.

SCENE SIXTEEN

(Later, Day Seven: Lounge)

HAPPY: Talk to me.

FULLER: What should I say? *(Pause)* You don't look good.

HAPPY: When your car broke down last summer, who gave you a loaner?

FULLER: You did.

HAPPY: Because I care. I'm built that way. And who helped you with the bank loan for that hernia operation?

FULLER: You did.

HAPPY: I'm not a bad guy, as guys go, eh Fuller? With my friends, I go deep. You understand that. Your pain is my pain. I don't want to see you in pain. You deserve better. I deserve better. Isn't that so? *(Pause)* Look at me, Fuller. I feel a little broken inside. *(Pause)* Why the fuck did you capitulate?

FULLER: I only told the truth.

HAPPY: Fuller...

FULLER: They're coming down hard, Happy. These guys are heavyweights.

HAPPY: Monteith dances on your toes and you go down. I know why. I know why. Your wife. You talked to your wife. Tell me you talked with your wife.

FULLER: I talked with my wife.

HAPPY: And she cried.

FULLER: Yeah.

HAPPY: And she talked you into giving testimony, because she didn't want to see you in prison.

FULLER: That's right.

HAPPY: And because I don't figure in with your situation, I'm just a piece of shit.

FULLER: No.

HAPPY: You're always being pulled by someone's strings. You realize this.

FULLER: We're all going through the same fucking ringer. *(Traded silences)* Yeah.

HAPPY: Yeah?

FULLER: I've family to worry over. I got responsibilities, Happy. I need to survive. Can't do time in jail. My ass is on the line. I didn't cause this shit. Didn't beat the Jew. My nose is clean. I got to tell the truth. I got to.

HAPPY: I thought we had a pact. Didn't we have a goddamn pact? Tell me we didn't have a goddamn pact.

FULLER: I need to stay clean, Happy.

HAPPY: Clean?

FULLER: Monteith says you've a record for past abuse. I didn't know you were on probation.

HAPPY: You made a deal, didn't you, Fuller?

FULLER: No, Happy.

HAPPY: Don't bullshit me. Tell me you made a deal.

FULLER: No deal.

HAPPY: They're going to put me away for a long long time, Fuller. Twenty years. You think I'm fooling? I'm expendable. Don't even cost a fucking nickle. I'm an example for the department. They're showing the press they can clean house. Is that fair, Fuller?

FULLER: No.

HAPPY: Don't patronize me, Fuller. I was your friend. (Pause) You got to show solidarity now. I'm running out of time. (Pause) Monteith showed me your deposition. You gave away the candy store.

FULLER: It was given under duress.

HAPPY: Let me tell you about duress. I'm in duress. You understand that? We're members of the same fraternity. A union of average American guys. Of tobacco and booze, the great late-night bouts at the corner tavern. We're a fellowship, Fuller. There are unspoken covenants. Don't break a sacred covenant. Turning me over like white trash won't do. Don't play the black scarecrow. We're joined at the hip, man. You go nowhere without me. I go down, you go down. You get orders from me. We're still brethren.

FULLER: Aguneir's dead.

HAPPY: I know.

FULLER: What do you want me to do?

HAPPY: Meet with my attorney.

FULLER: To what purpose?

HAPPY: He has a scheme.

FULLER: Come on, Happy. They got us cornered. They have my deposition.

HAPPY: You can countermand it.

FULLER: No.

HAPPY: Shit.

FULLER: Hey...

HAPPY: Hey, weasel.

FULLER: My attorney put me under wraps.

HAPPY: We've got to talk, Fuller. There's no other way. Put out for me. Listen to me. Come downstairs. Right now. I'll buy you lunch. My guy's at the restaurant waiting. Talk to him for one hour. One fucking hour. No pressure. I promise. We're going to walk out free men.

FULLER: Happy, what's the use?

HAPPY: There's an angle. My lawyer's got an angle. Just come with me, damnit. We can fight this with an appeal. We'll go after them. This thing can be fought. But I can't do it alone. Do you understand, Fuller. I can't do it alone.

FULLER: I was promised immunity.

HAPPY: You got immunity?

FULLER: Yeah.

HAPPY: You fucking scumbag.

FULLER: They forced it on me.

HAPPY: Look what's going down. Look. Look. Shit. Hey, Fuller...you know...look, friend...don't shit me...Fuller, come with me right now...

FULLER: I can't.

HAPPY: You got to help me, 'cause no one else can. I'll buy you lunch. Come on. Fuller.... (Pause) Look, sweetheart, I'm running out of time. My lawyer's going to fix everything. For you and for me. Our friendship's at stake and I'm getting angry and nasty and so fucking upset, like I'm getting an ulcer right now waiting each minute you dick around here, like I don't enjoy getting the shaft from my friend, my colleague, my subordinate, like it's time to join the goddamn rank and file, you and me, tight and proud, like don't play Judas Asshole, you little son-of-a-bitch, 'cause you know all hell will break loose on you before you can say purple Uncle Remus.

FULLER: Happy, you need more help than I can give.

HAPPY: Damnit, save my ass!

FULLER: I've tried.

HAPPY: Fuller...read my lips...I'll kill you, if you fuck me up. I swear to God. I'll kill you. Don't walk away from me. Don't play moral high-road shit. Just come with me. Just get in the fucking elevator and eat your goddamn tuna salad with my lawyer downstairs. Understand? Get your hat and coat and come with me to the elevator. Capice? *(Pause)* Fuller, my blood's boiling and I'm about to burst. I'll count to three. Slowly. With all the fucking dignity I can muster. *(Pause)* One. Two. Three. *(Silence)* Fuller, I'm going to count once more. Out of respect to your dear wife. *(Pause)* One. Two. *(Slugs* FULLER *in face.* FULLER *hits the floor.)* Get up, Fuller, and get your silly hat and coat. Don't waste a second of my precious time.

SCENE SEVENTEEN

(Day Eight: Lounge – Dimly lit)

HAPPY: I left the pizza in the oven, because I couldn't stand being in the house alone. Her car was still in the driveway. I waited. She came out with Ginger. They drove away after they caught a glimpse of me. *(Pause)* No note. No explanation. Nothing. *(Pause)* I went up to the bedroom and packed all my things. Took them outside on the front lawn. Bawled like a baby. Poured gasoline. Lit it. Blazed like a great inferno. Billows of smoke. Spirits in the sky. Neighbors ran out to watch. I went back inside to get the drapes off the windows. Poured gasoline. Lit it. *(Pause)* I burned my wallet and my shoes and every family photograph. *(Pause)* Went back inside. Smoke was pushing out of the oven. Phoned the authorities. Forgot my address. Got in the car. Knocked over the garbage cans. Drove to the highway. Went back over a dozen years. Saw my wife's first car. The Plymouth. By the shoulder of the road. Her high hemline of her skirt. Her legs. Her flat tire. Her voice. I jacked up her car. Asked her to dinner. Asked her to marry me. I fixed her tire. *(Pause)* When Ginger was born, we knew we were in love. *(Pause)* I drove to the pawn shop, with her shitty silverware and the Sony Trinitron. It was a place where no permit is necessary. I already had bullets. I bought a sandwich. I loaded the gun. *(Pause)* I waited for Joyce to return.

SCENE EIGHTEEN

(Day Nine: CORTEZ*'s room)*

FULLER: Any further questions?

CORTEZ: No.

FULLER: I've spoken to your colleagues at Harvard and they're to receive you in a private ceremony. A solution, we think. I gather you will leave the country after the trip to the college. Is there any other country in South America where you feel safe?

CORTEZ: I was thinking of France.

FULLER: Let me arrange a review board to assist you. I've completed your report. We appreciate your cooperation.

CORTEZ: *(After a silence)* I have compromised myself.

FULLER: Hardly.

CORTEZ: I did. There are things I cannot stand. I must push on. I'll have to pay for this later.

FULLER: You were undermined, Miss Cortez. We acted unfairly.

CORTEZ: You're quite different from Logan.

FULLER: It's the nature of a man's diet. A man's moral center. A man needs good influences. Like you, I have compromised myself. We are similar. I like your writing, Miss Cortez. You champion a good cause, in your own way. Your prose is vigorous, challenging, on target. Poor people need you. With the sweep of the Reagan years, you scare many flag wavers. Well, now you're free. Our borders are open. Enjoy New York. I apologize for the various hardships and misunderstandings incurred here. Your papers and visa are on the table. *(Pause)* Miss Cortez?

CORTEZ: *(Collecting her papers)* Neither you nor I are invincible. We find comfort in our respective pragmatism.

FULLER: Do we? *(Pause)* It's important to be realistic in the world we inhabit.

CORTEZ: Where is Mr. Logan?

FULLER: Why do you ask?

CORTEZ: I've something to tell him.

FULLER: I'm afraid that will have to wait.

CORTEZ: Why?

FULLER: This morning Mr. Logan shot himself with a revolver to his temple.

END OF PLAY

MINK SONATA

ORIGINAL PRODUCTION

BACA Downtown, Brooklyn NY, first performance 12 September 1986:

CATHERINE . . . . Victoria Boothby
RODNEY . . . . Randy Phillips
ROBERTA and BLAKE . . . . Gordana Rashovich

Director . . . . Allan Havis

CHARACTERS

ROBERTA—*A girl in her late twenties, slender, delicate with dark hollow eyes. She lives at home with her parents, and has a history of hospitalization. Her voice ranges from great tension to more muted, flat tones. There is much innocence to her movements and expressions. She also plays the cello.*

CATHERINE—ROBERTA'*s mother. An elegant southern-bred woman in her early fifties. She is fastidious, mannered, coy, and clever. Her conceits are plentiful, as are her homilies. She goes into personal campaigns to exert her will. To her credit, she is a sincere Catholic. She fears that she may lose her husband one last time.*

RODNEY—ROBERTA'*s father. A short, balding man around sixty. He is affable, off beat, a drinker, a practiced speaker – by profession, a political media consultant. His disposition fluctuates between genuine concern for others to rich executive aloofness. His lust is clumsy and paternal.*

BLAKE—ROBERTA'*s alter ego. She is stylish, self-confident, and very attractive. In image and attitude, she is the direct opposite to* ROBERTA.

SETTING

A large, rambling west side apartment in New York City.

PRODUCTION NOTES

ROBERTA and BLAKE are played by the same actress.

The play begins with a Prologue, with the three actors in white masks taking part in three imaginary photo sessions. They pose together with RODNEY in the middle. The Prologue should last no longer than one minute. Music for prologue might be foreign percussion or environmental music of an abstract nature.

To allow for the elaborate costume changes between BLAKE/ROBERTA, rear-screen projection and images of a woman against a screen of stretch fabric (seeing relief of her hands, breasts, and face etc. in motion) are suggested: silhouettes of a woman playing a cello in frenzy, of a woman holding up the see-through masks and turning to one over the other (as if rejecting one mask), and of a man and woman coming together for an embrace.

For the scene in Act One where BLAKE and ROBERTA talk to each other, it is suggested that the actress address children's dolls to represent surrogates of BLAKE and ROBERTA. The actress might wear a mask for half of the scene (as well as stay with the dolls for half of the scene) until she moves to speak into an imaginary mirror facing the audience. On the line, "You mustn't be harsh," the actress might talk over a pre-recorded tape with her voice saying the same line – as if an echo were heard.

Solo cello music from Bach is suggested to link the scenes together between and during blackouts. Sinatra music may be heard at the start-up of Act Two, Scene One. The song itself should be romantic and melancholic.

ACT ONE

SCENE ONE

(From her bedroom, CATHERINE—*still dressing herself—joins* RODNEY *in the living room.* RODNEY *is reading on the couch.)*

CATHERINE: *(Rushed)* Yes, in an hour. We're supposed to have dinner with the Farrows. It's theme night at Harriet's.

RODNEY: Harriet again? What shall I wear?

CATHERINE: Anything but your red blazer. You wore that last time.

RODNEY: Is Roberta coming?

CATHERINE: No.

RODNEY: *(Innocently)* Why not?

CATHERINE: Her little pets are crapping everywhere.

RODNEY: Oh?

CATHERINE: They've soiled every rug in here, Rodney.

RODNEY: Doesn't the girl vacuum?

CATHERINE: My priceless Belgium rugs, Rodney. *(Turning from a full length mirror)* I won't have it in my house!

RODNEY: Calm down, Catherine. I'll discuss it with her.

CATHERINE: *(Still fuming)* Damnit! They'll kick us out of the co-op if this continues! Word has gotten out.

RODNEY: That's not a problem.

CATHERINE: She's the oldest boarding school girl in the world. No real maturity. No friends. No dates. A complete failure.

RODNEY: *(Kindly)* Were you fighting today? *(Silence; gets up)* I'd like a brandy.

CATHERINE: I'd like her pregnant. I don't like lesbians for prep girls.

RODNEY: Many girls may seem that way.

CATHERINE: She can't hide it from me. The odd, vacant way she stares. Her bizarre make-up. She keeps changing her style of clothes. Haven't you noticed?

RODNEY: It's her age, darling. Wait until her thirtieth birthday.

CATHERINE: Lesbians are never happy.

RODNEY: What did you do with the brandy?

CATHERINE: They don't have real lives. They connive. They keep cats and birds and hide away in rent control apartments in Chelsea. And they have churches and doctors for themselves with spurious mailing lists. They do, Rodney, they do. I ran into Updike, the writer, at my doctor's. We talked. He says it's all true. And Rodney, he said it was your fault. *(Sudden switch)* My thyroid's acting up. Come see.

RODNEY: *(Approaching, with a gentle touch)* Is it? *(Pause)* So you met Updike?

CATHERINE: I did.

RODNEY: Is his daughter a lesbian?

CATHERINE: He didn't say. *(Pause)* I don't think I'm hysterical. It's just that I...I love Roberta very much. You'd think she'd realize this. I shower her with love and affection. Isn't that so, Rodney?

RODNEY: Yes, Catherine.

CATHERINE: And not a recent love. A love which flowered over the years. *(Affectionate caresses to RODNEY)* We should fly away, take a long vacation.

RODNEY: You know I don't want one.

CATHERINE: Just the two of us.

RODNEY: My work won't allow us.

CATHERINE: Our marriage calls for it.

RODNEY: It is my fault. I've probably been remiss.

CATHERINE: Then let's find her a fabulous place to live.

RODNEY: You know how fragile she is, Catherine.

CATHERINE: Why don't we buy her a Samurai sword or a Saturday Night Special?

RODNEY: Don't be absurd tonight.

CATHERINE: Was I being absurd? *(Kisses* RODNEY *playfully)* Then let us move. Leave her this apartment. She can have the darling rugs.

RODNEY: But I entertain here.

CATHERINE: There are suites everywhere in town. Or we could even leave the city. I don't care for New York any longer. I dislike all our neighbors. The elevators decapitate. The electrical wiring is in Swahili. The night doorman has scurvy.

(ROBERTA, having entered from her bedroom, interrupts.)

ROBERTA: He's a decent, respectable doorman.

CATHERINE: Then why does he wrap his trouser belt around like a Mexican bandit? And why does he always drink from a paper bag?

ROBERTA: He's eccentric, Catherine. Everyone's eccentric in this building.

CATHERINE: Yes, I can believe that. Roberta, do you want this apartment all to yourself?

ROBERTA: Why do you ask?

CATHERINE: Your father and I were thinking about moving across the river.

RODNEY: But I entertain here.

CATHERINE: Stay out of this Rodney.

ROBERTA: But we're New Yorkers, Catherine.

CATHERINE: There are New Yorkers in Nicaragua. We could live in Saddle River. Wouldn't a garden be nice? Raise tomatoes, turnips...

RODNEY: *(Mock conspiratorial, to* ROBERTA) Humor her. *(Crosses to his bedroom)* If you'll excuse me, I'll get ready for Harriet's.

ROBERTA: Can I go with you?

CATHERINE: No, dear.

ROBERTA: Why not?

CATHERINE: Couples only. So sorry.

ROBERTA: I don't want to be alone this evening.

CATHERINE: Play your cello.

ROBERTA: Catherine, don't be cutting.

CATHERINE: I keep insisting you try to make some friends. Friends keep us happy. Let's make an effort to be social! Take up ballroom dancing, Roberta. *(They exchange looks carefully.)* Expect us home early...but don't wait up for us. *(Abruptly)* Did you buy the anti-pasto?

ROBERTA: No.

CATHERINE: What about all the chick peas in the fridge?

ROBERTA: For the minks.

CATHERINE: Is that what makes them crap so much?

ROBERTA: No, it's your interior decorating.

CATHERINE: Don't be cute darling. It makes you fetching. I urge you to get these shitty beasts out of the house in 48 hours. Or else...

ROBERTA: Or else what?

CATHERINE: A plague will descend upon us from the Bible. *(Pause)* When are you getting a husband?

ROBERTA: Never.

CATHERINE: Marriage would elevate you to great heights.

ROBERTA: I don't like heights.

CATHERINE: Nor do I. At least we agree about some things.

ROBERTA: We agree about Rodney.

CATHERINE: Do we? *(Pause)* I'm going to throw you on the auction block someday, young lady.

ROBERTA: Why must I marry?

CATHERINE: Life calls for marriage. Your grandmother didn't want a husband but wasn't unhappy. She ran the marriage like a little boutique. *(Pause)* No, I never met a happy spinster. One day you'll wear my wedding dress. It's so wonderfully sheer. We'll take in the bust and improve the hips. Fill out your valleys. And the veil...

ROBERTA: Weddings are so depressing.

CATHERINE: Mine wasn't. Your father was the loveliest bridegroom.

ROBERTA: I can imagine.

CATHERINE: Aren't you seeing someone? That dire Jewish violinist from Philadelphia?

ROBERTA: I'm in love with the dumbwaiter.

CATHERINE: One day you'll wear my gown, darling. You will become a bride in full regalia.

ROBERTA: You scare me, Catherine.

CATHERINE: As you scare me, darling. Which proves we're related. If you stop scaring me, I'll stop scaring you. *(New smile)* Companionship, I cannot stress that enough.

ROBERTA: I have my cello.

CATHERINE: Which do you really prefer, little Cinderella? Linseed oil for your cello, or men's cologne?

ROBERTA: Animal manure.

CATHERINE: Why must you be contrary?

ROBERTA: I can't stop myself.

CATHERINE: It's a miracle that you can keep up with the orchestra.

ROBERTA: Yes, it's a miracle.

CATHERINE: I must get ready for tonight. *(Trying to excuse herself)* Do clean up your bedroom. And the newspapers in the cages.

ROBERTA: Yes, Catherine. *(Eye contact holding)* You spoil every Christmas.

CATHERINE: I'm very fond of Christmas. Don't we always pick out the grandest tree for the living room? Don't we go carolling? What would you like for Christmas, darling?

ROBERTA: A gargoyle from Prague.

CATHERINE: *(Deadpan)* But Roberta, we got that for you last year.

ROBERTA: Leave me alone.

CATHERINE: Is this our thanks for sending you to an epicurean boarding school?

ROBERTA: I don't know, Catherine.

CATHERINE: You happen to be a beautiful girl. Why must you punish us like this?

ROBERTA: I hate sex.

CATHERINE: Yes, I know.

ROBERTA: You don't know.

CATHERINE: It's so simple really. You bring flowers. He brings wine.

ROBERTA: When I think of it, I hear the gnawing of little bony teeth.

CATHERINE: Well darling. You'll have to think of something more pleasant.

ROBERTA: The pounding of decaying flesh is rather unsightly, don't you think?

CATHERINE: There's candle light, or those novelty blindfolds your father's so very fond of.

ROBERTA: Your mattress creaks like a decrepit sausage machine.

CATHERINE: Do you really stay up all night, Roberta?

ROBERTA: I do. I require no sleep.

CATHERINE: You should sleep. You need your sleep.

ROBERTA: Sleep is brutal. Like sex. I'd rather sing a ballad.

CATHERINE: That simply won't do. *(Pause)* I don't like your innuendos, dear. I think you should start getting dressed and remove the charming bird's nest from your hair. We may have company tonight.

ROBERTA: I'm ill. Let me count the ways. Agoraphobia. Stigmata. Anorexia.

CATHERINE: *(Oblivious to* ROBERTA*)* I'm ordering drapes. The rodents go. Immediately. I want the rugs washed and your room fumigated.

ROBERTA: They're minks. They're my friends.

CATHERINE: I'll buy you a fur. Anything in my closet is yours. You realize this represents a mild behavior disorder. If you're depressed we'll get you lithium.

ROBERTA: The ancient cure for step-mothers was bloodletting.

CATHERINE: I'm your mother. Not your step-mother. I know you want to be rid of us. As soon as you toss your head, I know. And when you get destructive I seem to be right behind you. *(Silence)* Would you ever let me kiss you? *(Pause.* CATHERINE *changes strategy.)* We're supposed to have visited the Farrows, but set the table for four. We've company.

ROBERTA: Who's coming?

CATHERINE: A student of your father's. I really know little about it. Please make yourself presentable.

*(*CATHERINE *busies herself at* RODNEY's *study.* ROBERTA *exits to her bedroom. In a moment* CATHERINE *exits. Then* RODNEY *enters toward the bar.* BLAKE *enters from the other corridor. She wears clothes distinct from* ROBERTA.*)*

RODNEY: Can I offer you a drink?

BLAKE: Thank you.

RODNEY: How was your flight?

BLAKE: On time.

RODNEY: Didn't you have red hair at Amherst?

BLAKE: Yes. I thought another tint would do well.

RODNEY: I think so. You look absolutely delectable. Have you plans for the holidays?

BLAKE: None.

RODNEY: *(With briefs under his arms)* I read these things rather frequently.

BLAKE: If it's inconvenient I'll come back another day.

RODNEY: You really should have phoned my office. My wife makes a point of these things.

BLAKE: I can understand.

RODNEY: Though she likes when I work at home, we've a policy about visitors. *(Hands her drink. Silence.)* Exactly how did we meet?

BLAKE: You were visiting the college as a lecturer.

RODNEY: And I invited you here?

BLAKE: Yes.

RODNEY: That is unorthodox of me. You say you're a journalist?

BLAKE: Actually a political science major.

RODNEY: Where have you worked?

BLAKE: *The Farmer's Almanac.*

RODNEY: I'm not hiring at this time.

BLAKE: Perhaps if you saw my work.

RODNEY: Really...

BLAKE: *(Persistent)* I want to work for you, Mr. Alexander. I believe in you. I'm very good with cameras and lights.

RODNEY: Are you?

BLAKE: Let me intern under you.

RODNEY: You're most lovely, and I would be flattered to have you on my staff, but it's really not possible.

BLAKE: If it's my age...

RODNEY: I don't hire women, it's that simple. If I led you to believe otherwise, please accept my apologies. Stay for dinner. You did go out of your way to come here. We'll set another place at the table. *(He abruptly dismisses her, and begins to read.)* If you care to, why not stay for the holidays? We've plenty of room.

(CATHERINE enters with coffee tray and cups.)

BLAKE: *(Acknowledging CATHERINE)* I like your home.

CATHERINE: Thank you.

BLAKE: And what a stylish Christmas tree.

CATHERINE: From the Governor.

BLAKE: I do hope it snows. Christmas is such a joyful occasion.

CATHERINE: We love Christmas. It's the only time when my husband isn't at work. He never vacations. He schedules his heart attacks between election years.

BLAKE: Is it his Havana cigars?

CATHERINE: *(Solicitous)* Rodney, I've an ally. *(RODNEY is ignoring them for the moment.)* How did you like Amherst?

BLAKE: Very much.

CATHERINE: Our daughter went to Amherst. She's a musician. Do you know her? A prodigy at age four. She's won countless awards. So incredibly gifted. *(Shows photo of RODBERTA on mantle)* As a child she walked up to a cello and began playing like a master. How frightened we were. What powers she possessed. Like Casals she could butcher the instrument or torture an audience. The darling girl plays for keeps.

SCENE TWO

(Later that evening)

RODNEY: *(At his desk, doing his slow burn)* Don't touch my things, Roberta. My desk is impossible as it is. You know I can't tolerate confusion.

ROBERTA: *(Difficulty with her unfastened dress; slants over RODNEY)* My zipper's stuck, please...

RODNEY: *(Responding delicately)* There. Now leave me in peace. *(She lingers like a forlorn cat.)* What is it you want?

ROBERTA: Nothing.

RODNEY: Why don't you help your mother entertain?

ROBERTA: She doesn't need me. *(Silence)* I realize I'm not your favorite.

RODNEY: I never said that.

ROBERTA: I'm not from another planet, Daddy. Did you really think I was?

RODNEY: Never.

ROBERTA: Still...

RODNEY: Darling, we've company tonight.

ROBERTA: Get rid of her.

RODNEY: Don't be petulant.

ROBERTA: Why do you like this girl more than me?

RODNEY: Who said anything of the sort?

ROBERTA: Then why is she here?

RODNEY: I'm a lecturer at Amherst.

ROBERTA: What has that to do with it?

RODNEY: *(Still annoyed at the interruption)* We're just extending our hospitality to a visitor. After all, she is from your alma mater.

ROBERTA: Do you think I'm from the sea like Ondine? Or was a difficult birth under an alien comet? Am I an alien? You used to read to me from Hans Christian Anderson in so many voices. Remember? The old farting gnome dancing around with his young bride? And little Thumbelina?

RODNEY: Yes, I remember.

ROBERTA: Christmas is like a fairy tale. Have you seen I've decorated the tree? *(RODNEY's attention returns to the desk.)* I don't want to go to church this Christmas.

RODNEY: *(Not looking up)* Why not?

ROBERTA: Because I'm lewd.

RODNEY: No, darling.

ROBERTA: Oh, but I am. I cook soup lewder than anyone. That's what Catherine thinks. I can read her thoughts. *(Sits on his desk like a teenager)* I think you're lewd.

RODNEY: *(Looking up)* Why?

ROBERTA: Look at your soup. *(Pause)* You remind me of Evelyn Waugh with a Brooklyn accent.

RODNEY: I've lost my Brooklyn accent. And stay off my desk, Roberta.

ROBERTA: I'll never marry you, Daddy.

RODNEY: Why are you acting so strange tonight?

ROBERTA: Maybe your daughter is confused.

RODNEY: Why are you confused?

ROBERTA: *(Sweetly)* I've been out of the hospital less than a year.

RODNEY: It's time I stop doing somersaults when you cry for me.

ROBERTA: I used to cut my hair every day like a superstition. Superstitious about the water in my bath. About the water in my drinking glass. I'm superstitious about swallowing sperm. I was deathly scared of tongue kissing. I thought men had pastel chalk on their little skin. I did.

RODNEY: You do this to amuse me. I am not amused. Your mother thinks we embellish.

ROBERTA: We do.

RODNEY: That we are overly involved with each other. You know she goes to St. Thomas every day. If only you could understand. *(Pause)* Alone at night, it becomes an unveiling. *(Pause)* Go put some make-up on. It'll do you good.

ROBERTA: For you?

RODNEY: For me. *(She kisses him lightly on the chin, kicks off her shoes, prances out to her room.)* She's so troubled. (CATHERINE *enters in a stunning dress.)* You look radiant, Catherine.

CATHERINE: Thank you, Rodney.

RODNEY: Where do you find these garments?

CATHERINE: Slumming through Bergdorf Goodman's. *(Pause)* Dinner will be ready shortly. One of those fifteen- second casseroles. How long is this girl staying with us?

RODNEY: It's up to you.

CATHERINE: Do you mean that?

RODNEY: Yes.

CATHERINE: Very well then. The guest room is ready. *(Pause)* Tell me what you want for Christmas, Rodney.

RODNEY: May I split my wish?

CATHERINE: No, that's cheating. *(Stroking* RODNEY's *hair from behind)* You must pay more attention to me at home. No more late-night excuses. You were such a flirt as a young man. Ever since your equestrian injury your posture has changed. You sit like a member of royalty. So erect. *(Pause)* I'm thinking of going into business, darling. You needn't worry. I plan to use my maiden name.

RODNEY: Why do you want to compete with me?

CATHERINE: If I wanted to compete with you I'd have an affair with a close relation.

RODNEY: You've had many affairs.

CATHERINE: Hardly.

RODNEY: Catherine...

CATHERINE: Can you count them?

RODNEY: Must I?

CATHERINE: I'm in analysis. We count in analysis.

RODNEY: Don't give me your sad dog looks, darling. No journals. This is silly. Your editorial skills—excellent they may be—are from another age. Nor are they warranted.

CATHERINE: I want to be a public person, just like you.

RODNEY: I don't like our being public.

CATHERINE: I thought about writing children's books, but who knows what they're reading? I prefer your kind of work.

RODNEY: You want to emulate your father.

CATHERINE: Maybe so. He gave you your chance in politics, Rodney.

RODNEY: And I am forever grateful to him.

CATHERINE: Father treasured your enthusiasm. Why not lend some to me?

RODNEY: Politics is not glamorous. It's a back-room affair. Always dirty.

CATHERINE: And therefore you'll tutor this lost debutante?

RODNEY: I asked for your opinion.

CATHERINE: What choice did I have?

RODNEY: You had a choice. You still do. Everyone has a choice. *(Pause)* And you made a good choice. *(Pause)* Why not send her in?

CATHERINE: Crash course tonight?

RODNEY: Yes.

CATHERINE: What's your hurry?

RODNEY: New agenda, no hurry.

(RODNEY turns his back to CATHERINE as she exits. In a few moments BLAKE enters, in loose, seductive clothes.)

BLAKE: *(At RODNEY's desk, clearing a space)* My first day on the job.

RODNEY: *(Not directly looking)* Come in with a dress.

BLAKE: A pants suit?

RODNEY: We start with a dress.

BLAKE: But Mr. Alexander... *(Long pause. She puts on a casual house coat.)* I'm ready.

RODNEY: Sit at the couch. We shall take polls today.

BLAKE: Polls?

RODNEY: You mustn't ask questions. *(Pause)* Begin with an interview.

BLAKE: Interview who?

RODNEY: The mayor.

BLAKE: The mayor? What do I ask the mayor?

RODNEY: Anything.

BLAKE: The mayor of New York? *(Pause)* Can I ask him about his personal life?

RODNEY: Yes. Stop toying with your necklace.

BLAKE: Mr. Mayor, can you explain why most of your friends are under indictment?

RODNEY: What does he say?

BLAKE: I don't really know.

RODNEY: He'd make you laugh.

BLAKE: Then I'd make a joke too.

RODNEY: No, don't. The mayor can't take jokes.

BLAKE: I can at least try to please the mayor.

RODNEY: He expects you to. Can you charm him?

BLAKE: I'll ask him into the studio for a drink.

RODNEY: Good. These last few weeks he's looked a mess.

BLAKE: Leave him to me.

RODNEY: What about the mayor do you want to capture on camera?

BLAKE: His cheap irony. He upsets me.

RODNEY: Why does he upset you?

BLAKE: Because he looks like a gay mobster.

RODNEY: Why does he look like a gay mobster?

BLAKE: It could be his tailor.

RODNEY: Anything else?

BLAKE: He has a habit of wincing.

RODNEY: And what can you do?

BLAKE: I'd lick the wincing.

RODNEY: How?

BLAKE: I'd drug the son-of-a-bitch.

RODNEY: *(Kindly)* I think you're a natural. *(Pours two glasses of brandy. He stops her from touching her drink, and then reproaches her mildly.)* There's a girl who follows me home after work. She's rather shy. I spoke to her before getting into my cab. She smiled rather passively. We stared at each other. I said if you're going to follow me...it will cost you dearly. It happened as if it were a dream. But I expect her now, casually, like the proverbial leopard in the corner. *(He nods, allows her to pick up her brandy. They drink together, cautiously. BLAKE sets her glass down, leaves the couch slowly.)* You may think the worse of me.

(BLAKE exits, then ROBERTA enters.)

ROBERTA: I don't want anyone touching you, Daddy.

RODNEY: Don't worry, darling.

ROBERTA: I can't help it.

RODNEY: You like to worry.

ROBERTA: Am I spoiling something?

RODNEY: Your mother wants me to pretend. How can I pretend? *(Drinking absently)* Maybe it was our days in the kitchen.

ROBERTA: You want me to move out?

RODNEY: Yes.

ROBERTA: It's because of Catherine. Why doesn't she move out?

RODNEY: It's time you lived with friends.

ROBERTA: I have no friends.

RODNEY: You're too old for finishing school.

ROBERTA: No more therapy.

RODNEY: No one said therapy.

ROBERTA: But I know what you're thinking, Daddy.

RODNEY: Do you?

ROBERTA: A stately mansion with rolling hills and closed circuit TV. Have you really tired of me? Daddy?

RODNEY: Darling, I'm at wit's end.

ROBERTA: Come to my window at night.

RODNEY: And then what?

ROBERTA: We'll elope. That's what you really want.

SCENE THREE

(Later that evening. At CATHERINE's door.)

BLAKE: *(Embarrassed)* I'm sorry, Mrs. Alexander.

CATHERINE: I thought I left it locked. You must be lost.

BLAKE: You must think I'm awful.

CATHERINE: Your room is two doors down. I do hope you're comfortable here. *(Pause. Seeing something in* BLAKE's *hand.)* May I ask you something, dear? What do you want with us?

BLAKE: Must I answer?

CATHERINE: Do you feel superior?

BLAKE: Hardly.

CATHERINE: No offense, darling. But young women are simply nauseating. *(Studying her sharply)* Will you sell copy to the newspapers?

BLAKE: No.

CATHERINE: You could make a lot of money. You know what I'm talking about. You ruin good families. This is a good family.

BLAKE: I realize.

CATHERINE: In due time you'll be given an office and staff. He'll give you more power than you need, or deserve.

BLAKE: *(Resisting)* I've something to say to you.

CATHERINE: You needn't.

BLAKE: Madame, I must.

CATHERINE: My husband is not your concern.

BLAKE: I had an affair with him at school.

CATHERINE: How delightful. Credit or non-credit?

BLAKE: I'm quite serious.

CATHERINE: Rodney likes a little recreation. It does wonders for him. Makes him feel frisky, like a puppy in the country. But understand, he cannot fall in love. We've been to all the therapists and circus wisemen.

BLAKE: He's in love.

CATHERINE: No, no. It's your vanity, that's all. *(Pause)* My dear, you don't realize we're married over thirty years. Our life together chugs on. You're the hitchhiker.

BLAKE: I love your husband deeply.

CATHERINE: I'm flattered.

BLAKE: *(Pause)* He told me you were dying.

CATHERINE: Did he really? *(Pause)* Do you believe that?

BLAKE: I don't know what to believe.

CATHERINE: I'm dying of boredom. Do I get any sympathy?

BLAKE: I'm not here to undo your home. I love your home.

CATHERINE: If you care for my husband, obey me to the letter.

BLAKE: How do you mean?

CATHERINE: You're such a sweet thing, really. *(Touches* BLAKE *quickly)* Sweetness can bring down an empire. You mustn't. Promise me you won't.

BLAKE: I promise.

CATHERINE: Now no more talk about Rodney. Trust me to look after your interests. I will not disappoint you. *(Leads her to her room. Crosses to couch where* RODNEY *is napping. She wakes him.)* Were you sleeping, darling?

RODNEY: Yes. In the middle of a dream.

CATHERINE: Roberta is failing. She's no better than her time away at the clinic.

RODNEY: I see, Catherine.

CATHERINE: We've become hostages to each other. She must leave.

RODNEY: You wish this every Christmas.

CATHERINE: I get depressed with every holiday. She makes me so sullen.

RODNEY: If Roberta moves her playing will end. Nine dead fingers. You must respect her cello. There's a rare and wonderful gift in her. What will happen to her hands, Catherine?

CATHERINE: Let them petrify.

RODNEY: Bite your tongue.

CATHERINE: I might bite you in a moment.

RODNEY: Admit you're jealous.

CATHERINE: I wish my father were alive.

RODNEY: Insouciance, he would say, like a parrot.

CATHERINE: You make a joke of his memory.

RODNEY: *(Caressing* CATHERINE's *hair)* I'm sorry, Catherine. But you're so very mean to the child.

CATHERINE: I'm not dead.

RODNEY: Who said you were?

CATHERINE: You.

RODNEY: To my contemporaries, you appear to be.

CATHERINE: How comical you are, Rodney.

RODNEY: Am I?

CATHERINE: And yet I'm devout to you. A subordinate. It's time to change all that. *(Pulls away from him)*

RODNEY: Very well, Catherine.

(Lights dim over them, and rise near ROBERTA's *bedroom.* ROBERTA *appears with some of* BLAKE's *clothes mixed in hers. The following dialogue is delivered with equal distance from both characters.)*

BLAKE: I so very admire your father. He can slay most any sacred cow without vulgarity. Only Jesus was more deft.

ROBERTA: Many people admire him.

BLAKE: Tell me the truth, Roberta. *(Pause)* Did you ever...

ROBERTA: No.

BLAKE: I'm afraid it's an involuntary pregnancy. Many astronauts gain in flight.

ROBERTA: I'm glad I'm dieting for I was once pregnant.

BLAKE: What's that sound?

ROBERTA: Minks.

BLAKE: *(Pause)* I could change your make-up. Stop your chin from receding. We can tweeze, add some eye shadow. Your lips are so thin and pale, like a child under cold water. Lift the hair off the neck. Such a lovely neck. We could, Roberta. I could be your little sister. We could shower together, pretend to be oriental, find the horse bridle. Move the hands. Drop blood on clean linen.

ROBERTA: You mustn't be harsh.

BLAKE: Of course.

ROBERTA: At school I was not jubilant. I was going to die for my period. The few boys I took home were all insane.

BLAKE: I once took home a walrus.

ROBERTA: Three feet on the floor if you please.

BLAKE: The boys I took home were not permitted to have oral sex. So I developed a taste for oysters. *(Pause)* Then a married man came my way.

SCENE FOUR

(Moments later. ROBERTA *comes into the living room with her bags.)*

ROBERTA: I'm all packed.

CATHERINE: So quickly, darling? I was going to help you.

ROBERTA: No, you don't.

CATHERINE: I hope you didn't take my good towels.

ROBERTA: Rest assured, I didn't.

CATHERINE: I'm so excited, Roberta. Such a big moment in our life. It feels like we're sending you off to summer camp.

ROBERTA: *(Acidic)* Do I get visiting privileges, Catherine?

CATHERINE: What sort of question is that?

ROBERTA: You've made a million rules for me.

CATHERINE: Of course you've visiting privileges. You're only a few blocks away. I'll take the cross-town bus to see you. We'll use the same dry cleaners. What rules have I made up? *(Helping her pack the last box in the living room)* Am I overbearing? *(Pause)* Yes. I must be. You don't deserve this treatment. Forgive me. Your father is so frail. The two of you have eclipsed my world.

ROBERTA: Am I the only one leaving?

CATHERINE: Yes, darling.

ROBERTA: She's moving in?

CATHERINE: Only temporarily. (RODNEY *enters in a smoking jacket.*)

ROBERTA: *(Plaintively)* Daddy!

RODNEY: What, sugar?

ROBERTA: That bitch is taking my place?

RODNEY: No one is taking your place.

ROBERTA: If I was a distraction, what will she be?

RODNEY: *(Approaching* ROBERTA*)* You were never a distraction. Why be so hard on yourself?

ROBERTA: *(About to cry)* You're making me crazy.

RODNEY: Please, Roberta. Be a big girl now. Catherine, would you please say something?

CATHERINE: It's your father's very own cadenza.

RODNEY: Catherine...

CATHERINE: Your father wants a plaything for the office. That's all it is. That's all it will be.

ROBERTA: I'll never love you again.

RODNEY: You don't mean that.

ROBERTA: *(Crying)* I do.

RODNEY: These are growing pains. We all go through them. How well I know mine. But the upsets fade. Something in nature heals us. Roberta, let nature take her course.

ROBERTA: I want to die.

RODNEY: *(His arm around her, consoling)* Cheer up. I hate to see you this way.

CATHERINE: Are the minks in their cage?

ROBERTA: No.

CATHERINE: Please lock them up now.

ROBERTA: I don't have to. They're all dead.

CATHERINE: Oh, did you poison them?

ROBERTA: Yes. You gave me the poison.

CATHERINE: Just as well. *(Pause)* I hope you packed your wedding dress, my poor darling.

END OF ACT ONE

ACT TWO

SCENE ONE

(Some weeks later)

RODNEY: *(At the bar)* Would you like some wine?

BLAKE: Bourbon.

RODNEY: On the rocks?

BLAKE: Please.

RODNEY: *(Bringing the drinks to the couch)* I'd like to set up an observatory on the terrace. Install a high-powered telescope. Study my neighbors from a correct distance.

BLAKE: That would be amusing.

RODNEY: Not that I'm a voyeur. I disapprove of voyeurism. Do you have a hobby?

BLAKE: I keep a journal.

RODNEY: What do you write in your journal?

BLAKE: Odd things.

RODNEY: Specifically?

BLAKE: Miscreant epitaphs.

RODNEY: You don't seem the criminal sort.

BLAKE: I'm not. Are you?

RODNEY: That's a difficult question.

BLAKE: Are you criminal?

RODNEY: If you mean for personal gain...no, I'm not criminal. My profession is another matter.

BLAKE: You pass as a white-collar criminal, don't you?

RODNEY: No. I don't wish to be. *(His arm around her)* Campaigns can be ethical.

BLAKE: I've never witnessed one.

RODNEY: You've become a cynic. Have I made you one? There are no true forms with our electorate. Hawks are doves. Liberals are John Birchers. A Neanderthal can turn progressive. For every position there are two candidates from the same cloth.

BLAKE: Which cloth am I?

RODNEY: A modern cloth.

BLAKE: What does that mean?

RODNEY: That you're durable.

BLAKE: I don't want to be alone, Rodney.

RODNEY: Do you think I'll desert you?

BLAKE: In time.

RODNEY: Let me be the judge of that.

BLAKE: Do you love me?

RODNEY: Yes.

BLAKE: Why don't I believe you?

RODNEY: I thought you did.

BLAKE: Just because you gave me an expensive ring?

RODNEY: I don't believe in ceremonies.

BLAKE: Why do you make me wear tattered sweaters around the house? And this peculiar perfume? I don't understand your taste.

RODNEY: My taste is peculiar.

BLAKE: Why doesn't Catherine object?

RODNEY: Is she bothering you?

BLAKE: Not any more.

RODNEY: Good.

BLAKE: It doesn't sit well with me.

RODNEY: Must we worry about etiquette?

BLAKE: But Rodney...

RODNEY: Is it wrong to love a beautiful young girl?

BLAKE: I feel dirty.

RODNEY: When?

BLAKE: When she's around.

RODNEY: Catherine?

BLAKE: How many wives do you have?

RODNEY: Quite a few.

BLAKE: I don't like your humor.

RODNEY: Because of her southern upbringing, Catherine doesn't let me enjoy my jokes. I don't expect that from you.

BLAKE: I'm often tired of your jokes.

RODNEY: Alright. I now know better.

BLAKE: Do I remind you of Roberta?

RODNEY: Not in the slightest.

BLAKE: But there is a remarkable resemblance.

RODNEY: Says who?

BLAKE: Many of your associates.

RODNEY: Let them eat cake.

BLAKE: They think I control you.

RODNEY: You can dance on my heart.

BLAKE: Would you like that?

RODNEY: I don't know.

BLAKE: One day I might try.

RODNEY: You wouldn't harm a hair on my head.

BLAKE: Catherine might.

RODNEY: She would never. She's condoned everything. Given her blessings, in fact. I'm very proud of Catherine.

BLAKE: Is that why you keep the bedroom door ajar?

RODNEY: This evening you seem to be on a fact-finding mission.

BLAKE: You're evasive, Rodney.

RODNEY: It's called...mystique. Hasn't Catherine oriented you?

BLAKE: I've heard the entire Rodney lecture.

RODNEY: Has she told you everything?

BLAKE: You snore, play with trains, stain your silk hankies, butter with your steak knife, have difficulty with your fly, use rubber bands when you fall limp, limp a lot, hide girlie magazines in a financial portfolio, take bromides when you visit your mother on her birthday. That was my briefing.

RODNEY: A sterling briefing.

BLAKE: She treats me like a long-lost relative.

RODNEY: You can repay her the kindness.

BLAKE: I will.

RODNEY: Is Catherine out this evening?

BLAKE: Yes.

RODNEY: Good.

BLAKE: You're feeling romantic?

RODNEY: Yes.

BLAKE: I'm not.

RODNEY: What a shame. Perhaps I'll take my nightly stroll, or play with my toy trains.

BLAKE: Who are you fooling?

RODNEY: Did you think...

BLAKE: A rape.

RODNEY: Out of the question. I've no strength today. And I take hormones. Depo-Provera.

BLAKE: *(Recoiling from him)* I'm not kidding.

RODNEY: *(Controlling his behavior)* Then I'll apologize.

BLAKE: All sorts of VIPs court you.

RODNEY: Are you surprised?

BLAKE: Yes.

RODNEY: Because I'm short and stocky? And part of the great turgid prose each election year? It's the bastard's need for philanthropy. I'm very generous with my time which makes all the difference. *(Approaching her again)* I love the delicate shape of your neck. I love the corners of your dainty mouth. I love your rough and tumble.

BLAKE: I don't like bedrooms.

RODNEY: Nor do I.

BLAKE: There are too many crucifixes in this apartment.

RODNEY: My dear wife sits on the bleachers with God.

BLAKE: Don't patronize me.

RODNEY: Whatever you say.

BLAKE: You'll have to stop drinking. *(Pause)* And stop these awful wet kisses. *(Pause)* And when you break wind, do it in private.

RODNEY: Blake.

BLAKE: Stop calling me that.

RODNEY: What shall I call you?

BLAKE: It's the sound of your voice.

RODNEY: I can't change that.

BLAKE: Try.

RODNEY: *(Softer)* Blake.

BLAKE: Again.

RODNEY: *(Fainter)* Blake.

BLAKE: All wrong. I'm not undressing.

RODNEY: I'll dim the light.

BLAKE: No.

RODNEY: We can fondle in the dark.

BLAKE: You mustn't touch me.

RODNEY: Take off that cardigan.

BLAKE: I hate men like you.

RODNEY: So do I. (*Hands touching her firmly*)

BLAKE: I'll hit back.

RODNEY: (*Absurd shift*) More bourbon, darling?

BLAKE: I'm not afraid to run away.

RODNEY: You are.

BLAKE: Just because you've crippled one girl, you can't cripple me.

RODNEY: Where would you go?

BLAKE: Back to school.

RODNEY: Admit it. You're unaffected by men your own age. I could set up a rent-controlled apartment on the east side.

BLAKE: No, I want something better.

RODNEY: There is nothing better, believe me.

BLAKE: You're a liar.

RODNEY: I'm a liar. So what. No one's offering trinkets.

BLAKE: Then what do I want?

RODNEY: An independent life.

BLAKE: No, that's not what you really think.

RODNEY: It's beyond words. Aside from the masquerade...

BLAKE: I don't want a doll house, Rodney.

RODNEY: (*Solemnly*) Marriage?

BLAKE: Perhaps.

RODNEY: A gauntlet?

BLAKE: Yes.

RODNEY: I thought so.

SCENE TWO

(Some days later. RODNEY's *study.)*

CATHERINE: Why are you showing me these pictures? *(Photos in hand)*

BLAKE: Aren't you concerned?

CATHERINE: No.

BLAKE: I wanted to report on Roberta.

CATHERINE: Why?

BLAKE: It seemed appropriate.

CATHERINE: My husband put you up to this. *(Hands photos back)* I don't care for pornography. Even with her clothes on.

BLAKE: She hasn't heard from you in six weeks.

CATHERINE: The separation will do her a world of good.

BLAKE: She's lost weight.

CATHERINE: Has she?

BLAKE: Thinner than ink. She's missed her period also.

CATHERINE: That's typical of her.

BLAKE: The orchestra's looking for her. Sometimes she doesn't get out of bed. The phone's off the hook. Yesterday I found her with the oven door open. I don't know your daughter that well, but I think she's in serious trouble.

CATHERINE: Roberta has a perverse sense of drama. If it's more grave, we'll just put her on medication.

BLAKE: It may be too late for that.

CATHERINE: It's never too late...for medication. Why take so much interest in Roberta?

BLAKE: Call it kinship.

CATHERINE: You've nothing in common with her.

BLAKE: It's as though I displaced her.

CATHERINE: Did she tell you that?

BLAKE: In so many words.

CATHERINE: She's very manipulative. I must caution you.

BLAKE: You discarded her like a stray.

CATHERINE: With a girl like Roberta, does one call the ASPCA? *(Pause)* Isn't she keeping company with an older man?

BLAKE: No.

CATHERINE: Perhaps she ought to go back to the mink farm?

BLAKE: She wants you to make a vat of soup.

CATHERINE: Whatever for?

BLAKE: For her consumption. Mother's soup, a miracle cure.

CATHERINE: Darling, there are no miracle cures.

BLAKE: Catherine, she wants to see you.

CATHERINE: I'm here.

BLAKE: You might pay her a visit.

CATHERINE: Do you insist?

BLAKE: I do. She's near anorexic.

CATHERINE: We can't have that, can we? Even if it's in style. *(Removes a fur from hall closet)* Give her this. No feeding required. Tell her to wear it indoors so no one can see her condition. *(Drapes coat over chair)* I wanted to collect precious stones around the world. We're absolutely mad about collecting. Rodney has his Lionel trains. I have my porcelain and china. Roberta, her scampy little animals. Our dinner service was always a problem. Something breaking every night. Roberta feeding her flock with my best china. Rodney's miniature railroad on my serving silver. What does one do when the entire family's obsessions coalesce on the dining room table? *(Stroking BLAKE's cheek)* Your make-up is quite lovely today.

BLAKE: Please don't touch me.

CATHERINE: Very well.

BLAKE: What have you done with my diaphram?

CATHERINE: Was that yours in the bath? *(Pause)* I used it to make strawberry preserves. I'm sorry, darling. I'll buy you another.

BLAKE: You enjoy playing these games, Catherine?

CATHERINE: Sometimes.

BLAKE: Perhaps you're sicker than Roberta?

CATHERINE: I doubt that very much. *(Pause)* Maybe I've too much time on my hands. I once took part in Rodney's office. Managed a good deal of it.

BLAKE: He said that your father started his career.

CATHERINE: There are many versions of that story.

BLAKE: Please tell me.

CATHERINE: I've no sense of history.

BLAKE: Your amnesia is selective.

CATHERINE: And so is yours. Do you employ mnemonic devices?

BLAKE: Rodney's cue cards.

CATHERINE: When we share these little secrets, I feel we forge a close bond. Even closer than your bond with Rodney. We are spoils of his ravenous appetite. Are we not in love with the same glutton?

BLAKE: How ugly you make it seem.

CATHERINE: Do I? I see only ribbons and bows, as I stare at his listless sleeping body.

BLAKE: If I were his wife...

CATHERINE: Perish the thought. Why would you want marriage when you already have access? Marriage is a series of unsightly stretch marks. I think I prefer religion in comparison. You can sense how vital a little string of beads can be. It's far better to marry God and tolerate His bits of neurosis. Dear girl, I've found faith and prayer the greatest power on Earth. One day you will partake. *(Pause)* Young lady, you are my own special friend, my dear contessa, my devout and loyal witness. Do as you wish as long as Rodney's happy, and peace graces our sweet home.

BLAKE: Thank you, Catherine.

CATHERINE: Who says its a man's world? If Rodney knew otherwise...though he's a remarkable instructor. And so clever at his business. It's not power, my dear, but perogative. And so you've permission to phone the party leaders, attend caucuses, fly ambassador, perhaps visit the White House. Wouldn't you rather be singing psalms?

BLAKE: I'm not staying for any more of it.

CATHERINE: Won't you?

BLAKE: No, Roberta's coming home this week.

CATHERINE: Is she?

BLAKE: Yes. Rodney knows.

CATHERINE: Again, I'm the last to know. She and Rodney must be telepathic.

BLAKE: You don't seem happy about it.

CATHERINE: I'm relentlessly hard on her. Yet it is her singular image which I love. Can you understand that? She can change faces at her whim, though never age. The years have been stern on us. Roberta challenged me with every weapon in her arsenal. Does she think she won by returning? I'd rather have a conflict in Heaven than an unmitigating migraine in my living room. No, Roberta has not won. *(Pause)* When she was a toddler she always had a peculiar way of sitting. That's a sorority joke. *(Pause)* How often I wanted to befriend her. To be her sister. To dress her myself. To throw all her hurt and pain away. To nurture her forever. How I encouraged her to nurture the cello and to make sacrifices to it. How I stayed with her during her first menstruation. Dare she forget these things? How often she sabotaged every blind date I arranged. How often I wanted to pop her little rodents into the microwave. How often did I visit the hospitals and clinics? Her illnesses blackmailed us. We paid too much, we never stop paying. And I pay more than anyone else. That's what's strangest about us. You see, she's closer to her mother than even herself. Down to rhythms and breaths. One pulse between us. My young lost Roberta.

SCENE THREE

(Some days later. RODNEY *and* BLAKE *are in his study, with* CATHERINE *sitting within earshot.)*

RODNEY: To accentuate would be a mistake. We could meet at the Biltmore, have drinks, go over the texts with Victor and the boys, and perhaps make a polite change or two. He likes you very much and I don't mind if you end up toasting to each other's health. Victor won't go further. I'd like you to wear something low cut, and comb your hair to one side. Show your beauty mark. You can kick off your shoes under the table. Let's give them a good show. There's much riding on this.

BLAKE: I can't make it.

RODNEY: What?

BLAKE: I'm sorry, Rodney. It's all over.

RODNEY: *(Turns to see* CATHERINE, *who shrugs passively)* What's wrong now?

BLAKE: Roberta's coming home.

RODNEY: So?

BLAKE: She calls me your whore of a mistress.

RODNEY: Excuse her humor. We all do.

BLAKE: She made me cry all day.

RODNEY: Why didn't you tell me this earlier?

BLAKE: I tried to hold it back. Catherine knows.

RODNEY: This meeting can't be postponed. Roberta can wait. Tell her to wait.

BLAKE: How can I?

RODNEY: Either you tell her, or I will.

BLAKE: She's threatening suicide.

RODNEY: If she tries anything foolish, we've no resort but to hospitalize her.

BLAKE: She'll tell the doctors everything.

RODNEY: There's nothing to tell.

BLAKE: She believes otherwise.

RODNEY: Who would believe her?

BLAKE: Do you really want to risk it?

RODNEY: No one threatens me. Not even my own daughter.

CATHERINE: May I say something, darling?

RODNEY: Yes?

CATHERINE: I saw her this morning. She's in awful shape.

RODNEY: That bad?

CATHERINE: Cancel the Biltmore appointment.

RODNEY: Alright.

CATHERINE: Meet with Roberta.

RODNEY: I will. Where is she now?

CATHERINE: Downstairs.

RODNEY: Catherine, is it safe to leave her alone?

CATHERINE: No.

RODNEY: Keep her occupied.

CATHERINE: I'd rather not.

RODNEY: Does she want to stay?

CATHERINE: It's gotten beyond that. Why don't you ask her yourself?

RODNEY: Quite frankly, she frightens me at these times. Should we call the hospital?

CATHERINE: I really don't know any more.

BLAKE: Shall I see her up?

RODNEY: Thank you. In the meantime, we should make some phone calls. *(To* BLAKE*)* Throw something on. You should look a little neater. *(*BLAKE *exits.)*

CATHERINE: I'm not happy about this.

RODNEY: We have to make some adjustments, Catherine.

CATHERINE: Do you want her to move back?

RODNEY: If the child's in pain, what can we do? You talked with her.

CATHERINE: She's greatly disturbed.

RODNEY: I see no other alternative.

CATHERINE: Then Blake must go.

RODNEY: Then she goes.

CATHERINE: But if Roberta is to stay, she must stop play acting.

RODNEY: How do you propose to stop her habit?

CATHERINE: We must find her a husband.

RODNEY: You seem indifferent.

CATHERINE: No, I still care.

RODNEY: Splendid.

CATHERINE: To hell with your sarcasm, Rodney.

RODNEY: Thank God you have our interest at heart.

CATHERINE: One of us must be the sober parent.

RODNEY: And the Lord assigned that role to you.

CATHERINE: *(Flatly)* He did.

RODNEY: It is a dubious distinction, Catherine.

CATHERINE: You're not going to have your way every time. You better pray she keeps a discreet silence.

RODNEY: I am praying.

CATHERINE: And ask for clemency, Rodney. Genuflect.

RODNEY: Must I?

CATHERINE: You must. Some devil's got you by the heart.

(ROBERTA *enters, wearing* CATHERINE'S *fur. She appears gaunt.*)

ROBERTA: *(In a daze)* Hello, Daddy.

RODNEY: *(With effort)* Hello, Roberta. What did you do to your hair?

ROBERTA: Henna. It'll grow out.

RODNEY: Come closer, sweetheart. Let me look at you.

ROBERTA: *(Frozen movement)* I have lice. Or ear mites. Rabid thoughts. Can you hear them? *(Pause)* Are you mad at me?

RODNEY: No, darling. Why would I be? *(He stands, approaches her.)* Give me your coat.

ROBERTA: Do you want to dance?

RODNEY: No.

ROBERTA: Do you want me to sit on your knee?

RODNEY: No.

ROBERTA: You don't know what banishment feels like, Daddy.

RODNEY: I think I do.

ROBERTA: It's a Munch painting hung upside down in Hell, where the walls blister and the fumes puss. It's a dish of De-Con poison in your school lunch. It's a black birthday card from Catherine The Great, with wishes none too pleasant. She weaned me on chloroform, though my recollection is excellent.

RODNEY: Darling, shouldn't we see a doctor?

ROBERTA: Heavens, no! They'll tap my head with their little rubber hammers. Write me a column, Daddy. Make me a star. We'll dine in Paris fashion, and fashion all night long. *(She dances a minuet.)* If you prefer the other girl, I'll be very bitter. Such surface beauty can't be everything. Good breeding offers more. We look for traces of Nature in Her truest face. We look for that seed which is not a spore. We want no weeds in our garden. *(Approaching* RODNEY) I don't grant favors any more. I won't bruise my knees for you. I shall not be scraped clean for my baby shower. I can never conceive. I'll not hide my moodiness nor my bowlegged walk. I shall not reproach myself.

CATHERINE: Maybe you'll grace us with a recital, Roberta?

ROBERTA: A recital, Catherine?

CATHERINE: I would love to hear you play.

ROBERTA: Look at my hands. They've grown extra knuckles. They move by themselves.

CATHERINE: Stop imagining things, darling. Your hands are fine. (ROBERTA's *fingers are now pulsating.*) Only a child pretends these sorts of things. You're not a child now. Don't worry us so.

ROBERTA: Wake me.

RODNEY: How can we?

ROBERTA: You know how.

RODNEY: No, tell me.

ROBERTA: Under the quilt, under the pillow, under my pajamas, under me. Rock me. Rock me. Catherine's out of the house. Another stuffed toy on my bed. Who is this creature, Daddy?

RODNEY: Don't rekindle bad dreams, Roberta.

ROBERTA: Who is this creature? Why is he touching me?

RODNEY: (*Seeing her physical discomfort, he puts his arm around her.*) You're quivering.

ROBERTA: I put all my feelings in a bottle. The safest place to put them. I'm only trying to be practical. In my wardrobe there are too many people. In my mirror there is a stranger. In the hallway Catherine rearranges the line of antiques. Why did she do this to me?

CATHERINE: Nothing has changed in this home, Roberta. It's exactly as it was.

ROBERTA: Even the windows are inverted. Nothing looks out. Where are the neighbors?

CATHERINE: Your hysterics are manufactured.

ROBERTA: My hysterics are your heirlooms. You can have them back.

CATHERINE: It's wrong, Roberta. I need your love. Isn't that a reflection of something? Don't rant on like some mad orphan.

ROBERTA: You're an accomplice to a greater madness, Catherine.

CATHERINE: I'm still an attractive woman.

ROBERTA: As warm as a marble bust. I am in awe of you.

RODNEY: Show me a sign of renewal.

ROBERTA: On my terms.

RODNEY: On your terms.

ROBERTA: You know my terms clearly.

RODNEY: Those terms are impossible.

ROBERTA: Try harder, Daddy.

RODNEY: Do you want us all to be crazy?

ROBERTA: Yes.

RODNEY: We are intimate, Roberta. Can't you accept that?

ROBERTA: She kicks and I rear. Enough, please. Take ten pints of blood. My head's about to burst. What a ghastly sonata, Catherine.

CATHERINE: Why don't you put on your slippers and bring down your cello?

ROBERTA: I can't play any more, damn you all.

RODNEY: You've never left home, darling. This was always your home.

ROBERTA: Why should I believe you now?

RODNEY: Because I am repentant.

ROBERTA: Show me.

RODNEY: Over time.

ROBERTA: Now.

RODNEY: You have my word, Roberta. (ROBERTA *exits slowly.*)

CATHERINE: You cannot keep fooling the child.

RODNEY: I don't intend to. We'll go back to a more perfect period. *(Pause)* Have I acted wisely?

CATHERINE: Isn't that rather late to ask?

RODNEY: When should I have asked?

CATHERINE: Twenty years ago.

RODNEY: You exaggerate, Catherine.

CATHERINE: You don't see any gravity to it, Rodney. I go to confession in total shambles. Where do you confess?

RODNEY: Confess to what? *(Pause)* I'm not a Catholic, thank God.

CATHERINE: Still very satisfied, how do you keep aloof?

RODNEY: The two of you frighten me. You know I'm frightened.

CATHERINE: I see postures and nothing else. *(Pause)* Rodney, you're an actor.

RODNEY: Only to entertain you.

CATHERINE: It will catch up to you.

RODNEY: I've gotten my telegram from Hell. Have you received yours?

CATHERINE: Yes.

RODNEY: We're due for a respite from our little ghosts. We could have played this differently. Why didn't you?

CATHERINE: I didn't care what you did out of town with her.

RODNEY: Your apology is in order.

CATHERINE: How can I apologize?

RODNEY: Let go of your rosary and mouth the words, darling.

CATHERINE: No, I cannot. *(Pause. Walking aimlessly.)* Our secrets have died and our plans have become slightly monstrous. Roberta has returned no older than yesterday. Her scars show only your handiwork. Nothing in the animal kingdom demands this much love and parenting.

RODNEY: Some children stay children forever.

CATHERINE: Are you one of them?

RODNEY: Forgive me. I won't be lenient with her. But Catherine, how are we going to change this child? She does what she pleases. She can't be trained. We knew this. Won't you please give me a sign, darling?

CATHERINE: There are no more signs.

RODNEY: I see many signs. Roberta will return to her music, relive her childhood, retreat. We can watch over her, give her shelter from the things she fears. Such is the order of things. *(Silence)* When you and I courted we had great expectations. Perhaps it's time for us to change. Twisted shadows pass.

(He kisses her. After a moment, they seat themselves in the living room—having set up a music stand and chair. ROBERTA enters wearing CATHERINE's wedding gown. She carries her cello and walks with some apprehension to the chair. She fidgets with her dress and adjusts her veil. She stares ahead vacantly, waits for coaxing. Silence. Finally she prepares to play. The bow lifts and we hear Mendelssohn. After a few bars she falters and freezes. Blood is seen spilling mysteriously from below the cello. Silence. Lights fade to blackout.)

END OF PLAY

THE GREAT THEATERS OF AMERICA

PLAYS FROM ACTORS THEATRE OF LOUISVILLE
$12.95

PLAYS FROM CIRCLE REP
$12.95

ENSEMBLE STUDIO MARATHON '84
$4.95

SHORT PIECES FROM THE NEW DRAMATISTS
$4.95

PLAYS FROM THE NEW YORK SHAKESPEARE FESTIVAL
$12.95

HIGH ENERGY MUSICALS FROM THE OMAHA MAGIC THEATER
$9.95

PLAYS FROM PLAYWRIGHTS HORIZONS
$12.95

Shipping is $2.00 for the first book ordered, and 25 cents for each book thereafter.

Prices subject to change.

WILD AND CRAZY PLAYS:

full length, contemporary & American

BATTERY
Daniel Therriault
$4.95

BEIRUT
Alan Bowne
$4.95

HARM'S WAY
Mac Wellman
$4.95

NATIVE SPEECH
Eric Overmyer
$4.95

ON THE VERGE
Eric Overmyer
$4.95

WALK THE DOG WILLIE
Robert Auletta
$4.95

Shipping is $2.00 for the first book ordered, and 25 cents for each book thereafter. Prices subject to change.

FULL LENGTH COMEDIES

COUNTRY COPS
Robert Lord
$4.95

GETTING ALONG FAMOUSLY
Michael Jacobs
$4.95

HIGHEST STANDARD OF LIVING
Keith Reddin
$4.95

HOUSE OF CORRECTION
Norman Lock
$4.95

THE REACTIVATED MAN
Curtis Zahn
$4.95

WHAT'S WRONG WITH THIS PICTURE?
Donald Margulies
$4.95

Shipping is $2.00 for the first book ordered, and 25 cents for each book thereafter.

Prices subject to change.

FULL LENGTH PLAYS BY WOMEN

BALLOON
Karen Sunde
$4.95

EMPRESS OF CHINA
Ruth Wolfe
$4.95

MOLLIE BAILEY...MOTHER JONES
Megan Terry
$4.95

...OMAHA MAGIC THEATER:
includes **AMERICAN KING'S ENGLISH FOR QUEENS, BABES IN THE BIGHOUSE,** and **RUNNING GAG**
Megan Terry and Jo Ann Schmidman
$9.95

WINDFALL APPLES
Roma Greth
$4.95

STARSTRUCK
Elaine Lee, Susan Norfleet Lee, and Dale Place
$9.95

Shipping is $2.00 for the first book ordered, and 25 cents for each book thereafter.

Prices subject to change.

ONE ACTS, SHORT PIECES and MONOLOGS

BIG TIME and AFTER SCHOOL SPECIAL
Keith Reddin
$4.95

THE COLORED MUSEUM
George C Wolfe
$4.95

ENSEMBLE STUDIO THEATER MARATHON '84
Bill Bozzone, Katharine Long, and David Mamet
$4.95

ESCOFFIER: KING OF CHEFS
Owen S Rackleff
$4.95

ORCHARDS
Maria Irene Fornes, Spalding Gray, John Guare, David Mamet, Wendy Wasserstein, Michael Weller, and Samm-Art Williams
$4.95

PLAYS BY JOE PINTAURO
$9.95

SHORT PIECES FROM THE NEW DRAMATISTS
$4.95

Shipping is $2.00 for the first book ordered, and 25 cents for each book thereafter.

Prices subject to change.

ONE ACTS AND MONOLOGS BY WOMEN

ENSEMBLE STUDIO THEATER MARATHON '84
includes **ARIEL BRIGHT** *by Katharine Long*
$4.95

FUTZ and WHO DO YOU WANT, PEIRE VIDAL?
Rochelle Owens
$4.95

ONE ACTS AND MONOLOGUES FOR WOMEN
Ludmilla Bollow
$4.95

ORCHARDS
includes **DROWNING** *by Maria Irene Fornes and*
THE MAN IN THE CASE *by Wendy Wasserstein*
$4.95

ORGASMO ADULTO ESCAPES FROM THE ZOO
Dario Fo and Franca Rame
American adaptation by Estelle Parsons
$4.95

SHORT PIECES FROM THE NEW DRAMATISTS
includes plays by Laura Cunningham, Laura Harrington,
and Sherry Kramer
$4.95

TRANSIENTS WELCOME
Rosalyn Drexler
$4.95

Shipping is $2.00 for the first book ordered, and 25 cents
for each book thereafter. Prices subject to change.

ANTI-NATURALISM

A manifesto against kitchen sink and trailer park plays

$12.95

BAL
Richard Nelson

HARM'S WAY
Mac Wellman

HIGHEST STANDARD OF LIVING
Keith Reddin

ON THE VERGE
Eric Overmyer

RECKLESS
Craig Lucas

THE WHITE DEATH
Daniel Therriault

7 DIFFERENT PLAYS

$12.95

THE BAD INFINITY
Mac Wellman

A BRIGHT ROOM CALLED DAY
Tony Kushner

DER INKA VON PERU
Jeffrey M Jones

IN A PIG'S VALISE
Eric Overmyer

IN HIS 80TH YEAR
Gillian Richards

KID TWIST
Len Jenkin

NO MERCY
Connie Congdon

WOMEN WITH GUNS

Six full length, contemporary American plays

$12.95

BILLINGS FOR THE DEFENSE
Calvert Parlato

ENERGUMEN
Mac Wellman

FEMME FATALE
Michael Wolk

SKIN
David Scott Milton

SLOTH
Bruce Post

WHITE MOUNTAINS
Bruce Dale